About the Authors

About the Authors

Writing Workshop with Our Youngest Writers

Katie Wood Ray

with Lisa B. Cleaveland

HEINEMANN

Portsmouth, NH

Heinemann

361 Hanover Street
Portsmouth, NH 03801–3912
www.heinemann.com

Offices and agents throughout the world

Library of Congress Cataloging-in-Publication Data
Ray, Katie Wood, 1964–
    About the authors : writing workshop with our youngest writers / Katie Wood Ray, with Lisa B. Cleaveland.
      p.   cm.
    Includes bibliographical references and index.
    ISBN 0-325-00511-7 (alk. paper)
    1. English language—Composition and exercises—Study and teaching (Early childhood).
  2. Language arts (Early childhood). I. Cleaveland, Lisa B. II. Title.
    LB1139.5.L35R39 2004
    372.62'3—dc22   2003017154

Editor: Lois Bridges
Production: Elizabeth Valway
Cover design: Jenny Jensen Greenleaf
Title on cover written by Billy Valway
Interior design: Lisa Fowler
Composition: Publishers' Design and Production Services, Inc.
Manufacturing: Steve Bernier

Printed in the United States of America on acid-free paper
10   ML   9 10

Contents

Acknowledgments

We would like to thank several people who helped make this book project possible.

Angie Leatherwood, Lisa's wonderful teaching assistant. Thank you for helping us with this thinking, teaching alongside us, and always pitching in to take care of the little details along the way.

Lynn Milner, principal of Jonathan Valley Elementary School, who so kindly supports both teachers and children, and who supported our work together right from the start.

Emily Wood, Lisa's intern from Western Carolina University during the 2001–2002 school year. What joy and energy you brought to our work together. Thank you for helping us see teaching through such new eyes.

Our families, the Brysons and Cleavelands, Woods and Rays, who were excited about our work together and understood the long hours needed to make a project like this happen.

Lois Bridges, editor extraordinaire and friend, from Heinemann. Thank you for guiding us through and believing *About the Authors* was an important project.

And finally, the authors themselves—all the children in Lisa's writing workshops the last few years who have taught us so much, and especially those from the 2001–2002 school year: Aaron Barnhart, Kayla Campbell, Colten Chambers, Levi Duffield, Riley Hannah, Jordan Henry, Meagan Hickman, Helena Hunt, Forrest Kerslake, Autumn Macemore, Carlie Mazurek, Ashley McClure, Cauley McClure, Cassey Parker, Sierra Perez, Tayler Price, Taylor Reid, Jared Rigdon, Joshua Shuler, Michaela Stiles, and Clay Wightman.

Introduction

"No matter what, just let them write every day. Even if you're not sure what to teach, just let them write. They'll do fine."

These were Lisa Cleaveland's parting words to the long-term substitute teacher who would fill in for her for the twelve weeks of her maternity leave during the 2002–2003 school year. And this is the belief—*no matter what, let them write every day*—that has guided Lisa's teaching in kindergarten and first grade for years. Even when she felt unsure about what to teach, she believed young children needed to take markers and paper in hand every day and explore the wonderful possibilities of written language.

We introduce this book with this belief because it is the point of departure for everything we have learned about teaching very young children to write: *no matter what, let them write every day*. We say it is a point of *departure* because it is a starting place only, not a destination unto itself. With lots of teaching surrounding them, we believe young children who have time to write every day can grow in all the important ways anyone who writes every day will grow. We believe, with lots of teaching, they can develop important understandings about what it means to write, useful strategies to guide them in the process of writing, a sense of form and genre and craft in their written texts, and a good beginning control of the conventions of written language.

We have written this book really for two reasons. First, we wanted to share with others what we've learned as we've explored teaching writing to very young children. What does this teaching look like? What needs to be in place in the classroom for this teaching to happen? And how does this teaching make sense in the context of five-, six- and seven-year-olds' writing? This book will address these questions from a variety of different entry points, including getting a writing workshop under way, preparing units of study, conducting minilessons, conferring, and assessing. And in Section 3, "An Overview of Units of Study," we share a variety of teaching resources for getting started that we hope readers will find helpful.

The second reason we wanted to write this book was to address perhaps an even larger question: Should we even be concerned whether very young children are developing in all these important ways as writers in the first years of school? Is this a developmentally appropriate concern for us to have as teachers? We have thought a lot about this question and we believe our thinking about it has helped us refine our teaching of young children in so many ways. Perhaps if we share this thinking, it will help others as well.

While we'll address the question of developmentally appropriate concerns from different angles throughout the book, we just want to say here that we aren't *concerned* at all that children develop as writers in all these ways. Nothing about how we work with young children has grown from our *concern* about their development as writers. We believe that curriculum that grows from concern has the potential to be curriculum that is shoved down on students who may not be ready for it.

Our work has grown, instead, from a *fascination* with their development as writers. We have seen again and again that when we get those markers and that paper in their hands, worlds of possibilities simply open up for all kinds of interesting development that feel natural and joyful and absolutely appropriate. We believe that the curriculum that follows these possibilities is a "shoved-up" curriculum, pushed upon us as teachers when young children show us what they are capable of doing. We hope that our fascination, and the respect we have for the young children who instill it, will shine through in every chapter of this book.

So, who are *we*? As we write this, Lisa Cleaveland is in her fifth year as a first-grade teacher at Jonathan Valley Elementary School in Haywood County. Haywood County is a mostly rural mountain county in the southern Appalachian Mountains of western North Carolina. Before coming to Jonathan Valley to teach first grade, Lisa taught kindergarten for seven years in another school, so she has experience with writing workshop in both kindergarten and first grade. Katie Ray is a former associate professor of language arts education at Western Carolina University, and it was in this capacity that she first met Lisa and became interested in her teaching of young children. For several years, we have put our heads together to think through the teaching of writing in Lisa's kindergarten and first-grade writing workshops. This book has grown from that thinking.

The *we* voice we use to write this book certainly includes Lisa and Katie in its antecedent, but we hope it includes our readers as well, all teachers of young children in all kinds of settings who want to think deeply about the teaching of writing into their classrooms. We hope that the possibilities we offer readers will transcend the differences we may see in the students we teach. We hope to get to the heart of what it means simply to be a young child who's learning to write and a teacher who's learning, every day, what it means to teach that child. We hope that readers of this book will find, as we have found in the process of writing it, that none of us will think *about the authors* in quite the same way again.

CHAPTER 1

Writing Workshop

A Happy Place Where We Make Stuff

It is late spring in the mountains where we live and the school year is coming to a close. Students in Lisa's first-grade class are spending some time in the mornings during this week doing "unassisted" writing, as required by the countywide assessment in grades K–2. For teachers of writing, the week is filled with lots of promise and maybe a little anxiety as we stand back and watch what students are able to do as writers all on their own. Lisa knows that her students should be ready for this week. They've self-selected their topics and made most of the decisions about how they would write things all year long in her writing workshop. They've had a lot of experience with what they are being asked to do, but still, every year we find ourselves sort of waiting around, looking over their shoulders and wondering, "Will all the teaching show up in the work they are able to do?"

As the children are engaged in writing for the assessment, we look over Josh's shoulder while he puts the finishing touches on his piece, *Mammoths* (see Figure 1.1). The tracks of Lisa's teaching across the year in her first-grade writing workshop are all over this piece of writing, as they are on most of the pieces the children produce during this week. As Lisa turns the pages of *Mammoths*, she says again and again, "Oh look, we talked about that a lot this year." *Mammoths* is an intricate mix of writing moves about which this seven-year-old is very articulate and can explain and ones he obviously knows and has internalized but isn't able to articulate yet.

With a first look at Josh's piece, we can see that this young writer is doing just fine with all the conventions on which we have traditionally

FIGURE 1.1 Josh's book *Mammoths*. (1) Mammoths, written and illustrated by Josh Messer. (2) Mammoths, written and illustrated. (3) Mammoths are the greatest animal in the world. (4) Mammoths lived in the ice age and mammoths have big horns to protect them from danger.

FIGURE 1.1 *continued* (5) The mammoth is eating some grass that is grown. (7) Look at that mammoth. It's having a drink of water. The mammoth is going to fall into the cold water. The mammoth is going to freeze. (8) I can see something. It's a mammoth. It's a frozen mammoth and the horns are missing.

FIGURE 1.1 *continued* (9) When a mammoth gets stuck, it's freezing. When the mammoths come back they see the frozen mammoth. (10) and now . . . The North Pole is a cold place. Where did the mammoths go?

focused in first-grade writing instruction. In *Mammoths*, Josh is writing legibly from left to right, spacing his words, using both upper- and lower-case letters, spelling many high-frequency words correctly, using his knowledge of both spelling patterns and phonics to generate unfamiliar spellings, using a variety of kinds of sentences and end punctuation, and using some internal punctuation as well. As a matter of fact, we could look almost exclusively at these issues of convention and pass Josh off as a proficient first-grade writer by our state and county curriculum standards. But we would be very disappointed if that were all we could say Josh knows about writing after spending a year in this workshop. We expect him to know a whole lot more than this, and he shows us that he does.

As we flip through the book, we notice all the other things Josh knows about writing that are evident in this piece. He knows

- One kind of text a writer can make is a picture book.

- Books of this kind have title pages inside their front covers.

- Books of this kind can have a mix of fact and story (a sense of genre).

- One way to begin a text like this is with a global statement about your topic (p. 3).

- Pictures in a text like this are often labeled (pp. 3, 4).

- A text like this often takes you back in time at the beginning (p. 4).

- A text can narrate what is happening in an illustration by using a progressive verb form—making it seem as if it is happening now (pp. 5, 7).

- A text can have an illustration that stands alone on a page (p. 6).

- The narrator of a text can speak directly to the reader in a command (p. 7) or simply as a way of engaging the reader in the moment (p. 8).

- The font of a text can be manipulated to make meaning (pp. 7, 8, 9).

- Two sentences can work together, with the second one stretching the first out and adding more detail to it (p. 8).

- A bold font can be used for emphasis (p. 8).

- A text like this often brings you up to the present time as a way of concluding (p. 10).

- Ellipses can be used to make the reader wonder what will follow (p. 10).

- One way to end a text like this is with an unanswered question (p. 10).

- A writer can edit a text for spelling (p. 2).

When we look at it this way, we see the child we hope to see at the end of a year of writing and writing instruction in first grade, a child who is obviously gaining control over the conventions of written language and who is also using language to craft literature. That's right, craft *literature*. Think about how obvious it is in this writing sample that Josh is making a piece of literature. He's not just writing something down about mammoths—*I like mammoths. I think they are cool animals. . . .* It doesn't sound or look like something you'd read in a daily journal. He's not just writing something, he's making something. It's a book about mammoths, his favorite animal.

Josh has had a lot of experience making books. From the first day of writing workshop in first grade, Josh and his classmates have thought of writing workshop as a time each morning when they get to make stuff.[1] They have things to work with—all kinds of paper and pens and markers and scissors and glue. They have stuff and they get to make stuff. It has to be writing stuff that they make, mostly picture books, but along

FIGURE 1.2 Girls at work making stuff.

the way they also make poems and letters and a few songs here and there, and by the end of the year, many of them will be making the grandest thing of all: chapter books (they're fairly awful to read, but they're *long*). But mostly they make picture books, books like the ones they read and study for ideas on how to make books.

Over time and with experience, we have come to believe that it is the energy of *making stuff* in a daily writing workshop that drives all our teaching with our youngest writers. From the very first day of workshop we fold up the paper, staple it together so it looks like a book, and then say to the five- and six-year-olds in front of us, "Come on everybody, let's make books!" It's this making of something that matters so much to them and drives their work across the year.

We have chosen to open this book with this one idea, the idea of writing workshop being a time to make stuff, because we feel so much else rests on this essential understanding. Think about Josh again. So much of what he is able to do as a writer begins with his understanding that when he is asked to write, he is being asked to make something and it should be something that looks and sounds like what he knows exists in the world of writing. It should be like something he has read. So let's open that idea up now. What's the difference, really, between having a time to do writing and having a time to make stuff with writing?

Making Stuff Is Developmentally Appropriate

First, making stuff is developmentally appropriate. Children love to make stuff and to help us make stuff. They love projects. They love to make cookies, build forts, decorate Christmas ornaments, make up games. They love the mechanics of making stuff, too, the cutting, pasting, stirring, and hammering. We use this energy in so many other parts of the day with young children. We let them build elaborate constructions with Legos™ and blocks, make funky art projects with dried beans and cotton balls and Popsicle® sticks, make up plays and perform them with all manner of props and ratty old costumes.

In writing workshops with young children, we have learned to use this same energy to fuel the writing. We present it to them in just this way: writing workshop will be this time every morning when we get to make stuff, or more specifically, we get to make really cool books. Next we show them some books last year's students made just so they can see what we mean and can see that it's something they could probably do themselves. And then we show them the supplies right away because we know the supplies are *everything*, the supplies represent worlds of possibilities. Their eyes light up when they see the supplies. You get a couple of scented markers in there and some sticky notes and colored paper clips and they'll be knocking each other over to get started! They love to make stuff, and we know this, so we use this energy for all it's worth, all year long.

The curious exploration children do when they are trying to make something, the trial and error, the joyful messiness of it all, is also so developmentally appropriate. Most children come to school with some experience with the inexact nature of creative play. Most of them have lots of experience with what it means to just pretend to be or do

FIGURE 1.3 Cele and Cedric share the supplies.

something. Most of them are comfortable with the approximations they make as they play and make things up as they go. We need them to bring this same ease and comfort level to writing workshop, this same willingness to explore and approximate and sometimes even pretend they know how to write. So by presenting writing workshop to them as a time when they get to make stuff, we create a context that feels familiar to them, a context in which they are used to taking risks. When we approach it in this way, we have very few children who, when they see what's set out before them and what they are being asked to do, think they can't do it.

Making writing workshop a time when children make stuff also opens up lots of room for them to make choices about exactly what they will do during this time. We know that developmentally, being able to choose activities from a range of options is very important for young children. The making of a book involves so many different decisions— what it will be about, the kind of paper and materials it will be made of, the illustrations, how it will go all along the way. Then there is also a whole range of ways to go about doing the work of a writer. With some teaching, the children will learn that during workshop time they may do different kinds of research on a topic, have a conference with a peer, read books for ideas on how to craft their writing, and more.

The children get to make all these little decisions along the way, and they find so many different ways to go about the work they do in a writing workshop. So, while in a bigger sense they are all doing the same thing at the same time during writing workshop—they're all making writing stuff—if you look closely at what's happening, you see there is a lot of different activity going on in the room. They aren't being herded through a set of predetermined activities. They are using the options they have to explore, figure things out, play around, and create, just as we know young children should be doing as they learn.

Making Stuff Helps Them Do Bigger Work

More than once we have shown other teachers writing samples that kindergartners and first graders have done in Lisa's writing workshops and then had them ask, "How do you get them to write so much? My students barely write a single sentence." And the simplest, most direct answer we know to give is, "Staple the paper together." Now, there's a lot more to it than just that, as we explain throughout this chapter, but the fact of the matter is, stapling the paper together and calling it a book makes a big difference in what children actually produce when they write.

Many children have lots of experience with picture books when they come to us, and those who don't will soon have experience because we'll read to them several times a day. They know that there are lots of pages in a picture book and that almost all of these pages have both writing and illustrations on them. So when we hand them this folded, stapled paper and say, "Here, make a book," most of them know right away that they should have something on every page, and those who don't realize this will realize it as soon as we show them what we expect. One of the reasons students write only a sentence when asked to write is because the medium itself—often a journal page or a single piece of paper with lines at the bottom and space for a picture at the top—suggests this to them. The book medium is a whole different suggestion entirely, and it causes them to do a very different thing with writing.

So right away students are doing bigger work just in terms of volume of writing and illustrations because we start them out making books with multiple pages. It's not uncommon for children to sustain writing for several days on a single book early in the year, especially when we enforce the finishing rules for filling up all the pages (more about this in the next chapter).

Now, you may be wondering, "Why do you start them all out making picture books? Surely there are other kinds of public writing in the world that children have seen—newspapers, magazines, letters, billboards, and signs." We have come to a place where we start the year with everyone making picture books for several reasons. One is that picture books encourage volume right away, as we've already said, but they also use both written text and illustrations to make meaning, and developmentally at this age, most children need to use both to communicate on paper. As they develop fluency with written language this will become less true, but at the beginning the illustrations help them make important meanings. Most of children's reading experience in kindergarten and first grade is with picture books, so this written form is the most familiar to them and this helps them know what kind of thing they are trying to make. And finally, because the picture book is a form, a container in which many genres can be written, we will use it later in the year to hold the writing of the specific genres we choose to study.

So, back to the idea of bigger work. As children begin the year making picture books, they are writing with more volume, but the work is bigger in another way, too. The *idea* of the work is bigger, the sense the children get of what they are doing with writing is much, much bigger. Whenever we think about the bigness of the work the children do, we are always taken back to Maggie and Larke, two girls in Lisa's kindergarten class several years ago. When Katie visited Lisa's class one morning, she sat down next to these two young writers, who were deeply engaged in making something. "What are you girls working on?"

They looked up and one of them said, "We're writing a series. It's sort of like *Frog and Toad* and *Henry and Mudge*, but it's about us." And then they proceeded to show Katie the first two finished books in the series and the third one, which they were working on that morning (see Figure 1.4).

The work is so big. The idea of the work is so big. *We're writing a series. It's sort of like* Frog and Toad *and* Henry and Mudge*, but it's about us.* The writing itself is sort of small in comparison, but the work is very big. And we see this again and again in students' work. Just like their attempts to build entire cities out of Legos™ and make spaceships out of empty boxes, it doesn't take them long to start making really big stuff during writing time. The writing may look small, but the work is big—just ask them to tell you what they're doing. Ask them and listen as Ashley and Meagan and Michaela explain they're making a poem "am-fology" called *As I Walk Through* and it's going to have "probably thirty-seven poems" in it when they're finished. Listen as Forrest and Joshua explain how their nonfiction book about space is going to have illustrations and facts in it that they've gotten from their research on the Internet. Listen as Cassie explains that she's going to give her book about her grandmother's death to her mom to make her feel better. Their work is such big work.

The key to believing in our students' ability to do really big work in our writing workshops is to remember they will do it like five- and six- and seven-year-olds. It will look and sound like five- and six- and seven-year-olds wrote it. If we can accept this, then they can do it, whatever the *it* may be. If we struggle with accepting this, we might need an understanding of *approximation*, which has more breadth than it has previously had in conversations about young children's writing. We have known for a long time that to understand beginning writing, we need to honor the smart, theoretical thinking children have to do to approximate spelling and other language conventions. Perhaps, then, approximation is also the key to help us understand and believe more easily in their ability to do very big work as writers at such a young age. Perhaps we feel the need to say that Maggie and Larke have approximated the work of series writers rather than actually written a series (but don't tell them that), but that doesn't make their work any less valuable and it doesn't change the intention of their work at all. They set out to write a series. They set out to do big work.

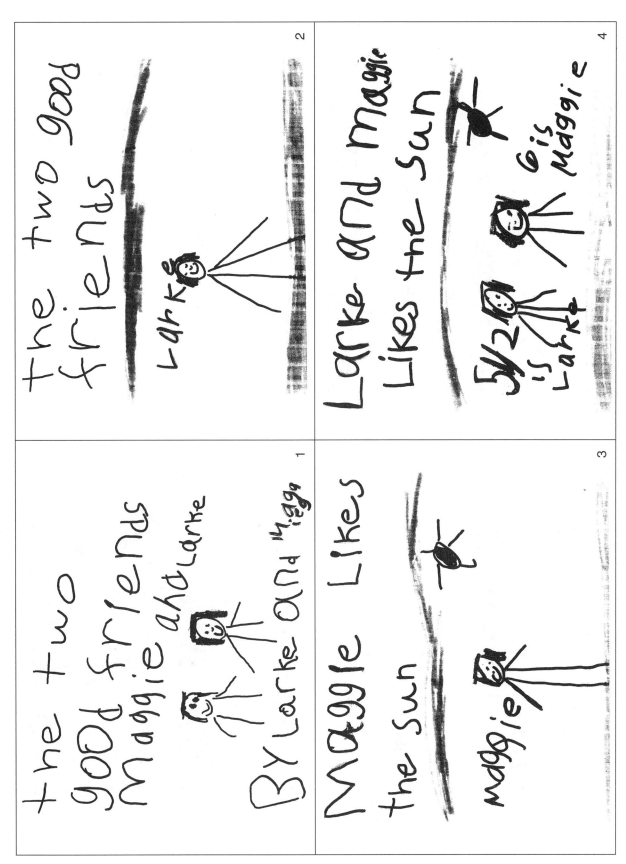

FIGURE 1.4 The Maggie and Larke series books, 1–3. BOOK ONE: (1) The Two Good Friends, Maggie and Larke by Larke and Maggie. (2) The two good friends. (3) Maggie likes the sun. (4) Larke and Maggie like the sun.

FIGURE 1.4 *continued* (5) Larke and Maggie both like the moon. (6) Me and Larke together. (7) Maggie and Larke love each other.

FIGURE 1.4 *continued* BOOK TWO: (1) The friends. (2) Me and Maggie went out to dinner last night. (3) We had fun. (4) At Wendys, I was getting my ketchup but I spilt my ketchup on my hand!

FIGURE 1.4 *continued* BOOK THREE: (1) Maggie and Larke are friends. (2) Larke and Maggie take dance together. We don't like the part where we have to put our leg on the bar.

Making Stuff Helps Students Read Like Writers

One morning as Lisa is showing students something about the writing in Libba Moore Gray's memoir *My Mama Had a Dancing Heart* (1995), Ashley interrupts her and says, "Hey, my book about my dad is written like that." Ashley and her classmates think of themselves as people who make books, so it's very natural for her to think of her own work as being like Libba Moore Gray's work. In their writing workshop, Ashley and her classmates talk a lot about people who make books. Early in the year they watch videos of Eric Carle and Donald Crews and Mem Fox. They study book flaps and dedications and they always talk about who wrote and who illustrated any book they are reading. They go to authors' and illustrators' websites to learn even more about people who make books.

Thinking of themselves as people who make books is the starting point for students learning to read like writers, the most important habit of mind for writing they will develop all year. Reading like a writer means that when you read, you think about more than just what a text is about, its meaning. When you read like a writer, you also notice and think about *how* a text is written, because you write yourself and you just notice things like that. People who cook a lot will notice things about food that people who don't cook won't notice. People who garden will notice things about plants, people who play music will notice things about music, and people who write notice things about how texts are written. They can't help it; who they are determines how they see the world. So when children come to think of themselves as people who make books, they begin to look at books differently. Everything they notice about how books are made becomes something they might try when they make them.

We'll never forget the morning Levi shared a book he was making and Lisa noticed something a little out of the ordinary. On the back cover of the book, Levi had drawn a circle and inside the circle there was an illustration that matched what the book was about. When Lisa asked Levi to explain, instead of saying anything, he walked over and got two books out of the Frank Asch basket, *The Earth and I* (1994) and *Water* (1995). He brought them back and turned them over and showed her that Asch had an illustration enclosed in a circle on the back of both these books. As many times as we had read these Asch books, we had never noticed that circular illustration on the back cover, but Levi noticed it and incorporated it into his repertoire of things he knew he could do when he made a book. He saw his own work as being like the work of Frank Asch, and this opened up a direct learning channel between Frank and Levi.

So many of the things we see that Josh knows about writing in his *Mammoths* piece are things he and his classmates have noticed in books

FIGURE 1.5 A child has placed her book in a bin of books with similar text structures. She sees her writing as being like theirs.

during the year and have talked and talked about. This is why when Lisa looks at *Mammoths*, it's like walking back through her year of teaching. She remembers so many conversations about so many of the things she sees there—incorporating features of nonfiction texts, like labeling; creating an ending that leaves readers with a question; speaking directly to a reader in a text like this; manipulating print to make meaning; using punctuation like ellipses to communicate with readers; and on and on. All these writing moves are things they've noticed in the books by the authors they love and admire. And of course, some of the more subtle things Josh is doing are things he has picked up all on his own, the sound and move-ment of writing like this, which he has internalized from reading on his own and from being read to by more experienced readers. But it all begins with Josh coming to see himself as a person who makes books too, just like all the authors and illustrators he encounters in his reading.

We believe so strongly in teaching very young children to read like writers. We believe that all there is to know about how to write well is found in well-written texts. And we also know that reading like a writer is the one habit of mind that will stay with our students and teach them throughout their lives. We want them to leave us knowing that the way to learn to write well is to study the writing of people who write well while you're writing yourself. They are young children studying Nicola Davies' and Chris Raschka's picture books right now, but someday they may be law students needing to write their first powerful legal briefs or concerned citizens desperately needing to write an editorial. And when they are these adults, they will have that lesson deep inside them that they need to read the kind of thing they are trying to write.

So, we have come to a place where we've decided, "With so much of our teaching depending on students reading like writers, how can we not get them making books right away?" For writing workshop, we start them all out making picture books because this is the mainstay of their diets as readers. We know that as they develop fluency, we'll expect to see more and more writing in these books. We know that as their reading lives grow to include other kinds of texts, we will expect them to begin writing other kinds of texts. We know that during the day, in times outside writing workshop, our young students will use writing for many other purposes—to record, reflect, sign up, sign out, gather, think, explain. But during writing workshop, they are makers of books and we build all our teaching around that identity.

This is probably a good time to address a frequently asked question: What about daily writing journals? In many primary classrooms, children are asked to write in daily journals because their teachers believe they need a place to explore and experiment, to actually try their hand at writing.

The expression often used for this is *freewriting*. Developmentally, we believe that when children are five and six and seven years old, freewriting is the only kind of writing there is! If the children are really producing the writing, then there isn't some other, more formal and polished kind of writing they will do, not on their own anyway. The reason young children's writing is messy and inexact and full of approximations is not because they're being sloppy or careless or "free" when they write. As a matter of fact, producing a written text *all by themselves* is quite an achievement of intellect and fine motor control. Writing workshop with our youngest writers is all about creating a space in the day when children are very free to experiment, explore, and approximate with writing. And for all the reasons mentioned in this chapter, we have decided to have them do this as they make stuff with writing rather than do it in a journal. A journal is not a kind of thing that they read, and we've decided the reading-like-writers connection is just too precious to lose on journal writing.

Making Stuff Helps Students Live Like Writers All the Time

One afternoon when all the other students have finished their snacks and gone back to other work around the room, Helena is the only child left still eating in the snack area. At one point in between bites, Helena looks up and says to Lisa, "Mrs. Cleaveland, I'm all alone." And before Lisa can even respond, Helena says, "Hey, that would be a good repeating line for a book: 'I'm all alone.'"

It's been hours since writing workshop, and it will be hours before the next day's workshop, but Helena and many of her classmates don't think about their writing just during writing time. From Lisa's teaching and the absolute everyday nature of the workshop, they are learning to be the kind of people who make books. They are learning that people who make books get ideas all the time, especially when they aren't actually writing. They are learning that people who make books are always "on the listen" for language that sounds fresh and interesting. They are learning, as James Dickey has said, that people who make books are people who "notice and are enormously taken by things somebody else would walk by" (in Murray 1990, 17).

In this classroom, being a maker of books is a very big part of a child's identity, as it is for Helena. Not only is she a maker of books, she is known as a maker of books with fabulous, elaborate illustrations, a maker of books with lots of animals in them, a maker of books that often have repeating lines and patterns in them, a maker of books who might surprise you with a clever ending. Helena thinks of herself as this kind of person not because someone has told her she is, but because she has made lots of books like this. Like everyone else in the world, she defines herself by the kinds of things she does a lot in life. In the classroom she works on making books like this every day, and so it's a very big part of who she is when she's there. But the thing is, when something is so much a part of who you are, you don't stop being that kind of person when you're not doing that thing. You think like that kind of person all day long.

Perhaps you have the memory of building or making something when you were a child—a clubhouse, a fort, a racing car for the box-car derby in Boy Scouts. If so, you probably remember being so consumed with the project that you thought about it all the time, even when you weren't working on it. You drew sketches of it on the news bulletin in church. You hunted through your dad's old tools in the garage, looking for things you might use. You went to sleep at night thinking about what you would do to it the next day. You became a person who was building a clubhouse, a fort, a race car, and while you were so engaged in that, this became a very big part of how you saw the world. And this is what happens when children become very engaged as people who make books. They think about this work even when they aren't actually working on it.

What is so interesting to us as we see students thinking about writing when it's not writing time is that it sort of flies in the face of so much of their other, quite natural, in-the-moment behavior. Developmentally, we see that children at this age tend to focus fairly specifically on whatever they are doing at any given moment. They sort of slam through the day with a rather joyous sense of "Now I'm doing this. Now I'm doing this. Now I'm doing this. . . ."

So how do they come to actually think about writing when it's not writing time, when this is not really their nature? First of all, the work is big enough to carry them through some measure of time. Because we have them making books, their writing is much more projectlike in nature, and it exists over time in a way so many school tasks do not. Also, we think it has a lot to do with the fact that having a time every day when they make books is just so darn predictable. They know it will happen at nine every morning. If, instead, the classroom felt like the teacher were making each day up as she went along, with the children never knowing what would come next until someone told them, then they would slam joyously through the day (if the work was interesting to them) but not get this sense of being a certain kind of person who does anything particular on a regular basis.

Related to this, if students have writing time every day, but that time is highly directed by someone else, then they have no need to think like writers outside of that time. When students are given a story starter or a journal prompt each day, they don't come to see themselves as people who need ideas for writing. When someone tells students exactly how everything should be written, they have no reason to notice and get ideas for their writing when they're hearing a bedtime book at home at night (Helena's mom told us she can hardly get through a book anymore without Helena commenting on how it's written!). For students to think like writers across their lives, to develop that essential habit of mind as writers, we believe we have to help them see themselves as the kind of people who write, and at this age we translate that simply as "the kind of people who make books."

Carlie joined Lisa's class in late October and found herself surrounded by all these little people who made books. When you're not used to those kind of people and you don't think of yourself in that way, finding yourself in their midst can be a little intimidating. You're not quite sure what they're all talking about and how they all know how to do what they're doing. But Carlie watched and learned and as children so naturally do, she soon joined in all the activity around her.

One afternoon after recess in late January, Carlie waited in line with her classmates at the water fountain. Quite out of the blue she said to Lisa, "We didn't do books or authoring or writing books at my old school. We just wrote on one blank piece of paper, and we had to copy from books." No one had been talking about writing in line at the fountain, and again they were hours removed from the actual writing in that day's workshop, but Carlie was obviously thinking about this new part of her identity and she was moved to comment on it. She had recently finished her book *America and the Two Twin Towers* (Figure 1.6) and we could see that her identity as a writer in a room full of writers was so strengthened by capturing so many important feelings in this book and then sharing them with others.

We are moved by the enormous implications of teaching like this. We are moved when we realize our decisions in the classroom teach students to think of themselves as particular kinds of people. But we realize that *all* teaching does this. If we told students what to do all day long, we'd be teaching them to think of themselves as people who should wait to be told what to do. So we embrace the people we ask them to become, people who make books, and we teach and teach into this essential identity.

Note

1. We searched for a more eloquent word than *stuff*, but we couldn't find one we liked!

America and the 2 Twin Towers

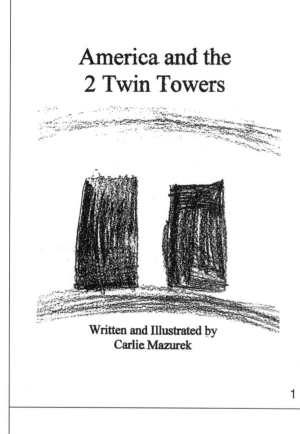

Written and Illustrated by
Carlie Mazurek

1

Did you hear about the 2 Twin Towers that fell down? That was sad.

2

They fell down in New York. We watched the news all day.

3

It was too sad.

Bin Laden is the one that planned to kill the people that was in the airplane.

4

FIGURE 1.6 Carlie's book about the Two Twin Towers.

There was trash everywhere!

America is at war and the Army is going to war and Bin Laden is hiding in caves.

5

6

Yes, they are going to war.

It was just too sad.

7

8

FIGURE 1.6 *continued*

It happened at September 11, 2001.

9

FIGURE 1.6 *continued*

CHAPTER 2

Work, Space, and Time

Writing Workshop Right from the Start

In early December, a news crew from our local ABC television station came to Lisa's room on a Monday morning to film a segment on her writing workshop for their weekly education feature. Not a problem, except that they couldn't be there until 10:30 that morning and writing workshop routinely starts at 9:00 and runs until about 10:00 or 10:15. The children probably could have adjusted—albeit a little grumpily—to moving to a later time, but five teachers from Atlanta were also scheduled to visit writing workshop that day, and they were coming at 9:00. The solution? Lisa and the children simply had two separate hour-long workshops that morning, one at 9:00 and another at 10:30. And here's the thing: the children were fine with this. They essentially worked all morning on their various writing projects and seemed quite happy to do it. It was very clear that by this point in December, these children were accustomed to working on writing during big, open blocks of time.

How do we get all this started? How do we create a time and space in our primary classrooms where very young children come to think of themselves as makers of books? How do we get them working purposefully at this for long stretches of time? These are the questions we want to think through in this chapter, but before we do, we need to answer another, more important question: Why? Why do we believe a daily, hour-long writing workshop is essential for our teaching of writing to young children? The answer to this question really comes down to a belief that two things are essential for children's development as writers:

experience and teaching. A writing workshop creates a space for both to happen naturally, side by side.

Children Need Experience with Writing

We believe that if children (or adults, for that matter) are to learn to write well, they need lots and lots of experience with writing. There is no such thing as too much writing if you are trying to develop yourself as a writer. The more you do it, the easier it becomes for you to continue to do it and the more you learn about how it gets done.

By the end of first grade, often two years into their school writing, we want children to have spent countless hours with pens and markers in hand and paper in front of them, making all the decisions someone who writes has to make. We know they will have to make these decisions like five- and six- and seven-year-olds, but still we want them to make them. We want them to have thought of ideas for countless pieces of writing in many different forms and genres. We want them to have represented these ideas with rich illustrations. We want them to have generated spellings for hundreds of words—wonderful words like *tyrannosaurus rex, camouflage, quenched, diurnal, sea anemone,* and *Central South America* (just a few of our favorites from last year) and, of course, ordinary words, over and over and over, words like *the* and *some* and *because.* We want them to have combined those words into a rich variety of sentences that ask questions, make emphatic statements, move a story forward. We want them to have made decisions about hundreds of punctuation marks, to have figured out how to begin and end all kinds of pieces, to have tried

FIGURE 2.1 Hunter works on a book during writing workshop.

things that will entertain the readers who read the things they write. We also want them to have used writing for a rich variety of purposes across the day in school—writing to help them learn and do other things outside of writing workshop. We want all these things that people have to do when they write to have become very natural, routine things that children are very used to doing.

The only way for children to leave first grade with this much experience is for them to have had time—every day over the past year or two—to hold pens and markers and paper in their hands and to write, as best they can, with their growing sense of how it all goes guiding them. So, first and foremost, the writing workshop is about making a time every day for children to get this experience with writing that we so value, much as we plan for children to have meaningful encounters with books each day.

Children Need Teaching to Support Their Writing

The other thing that the workshop structure affords us is the opportunity to infuse the time spent writing with teaching. We know that in many kindergarten and first-grade classrooms, instead of having a writing workshop, children do their writing independently in a writing center somewhere in the room. They may be required to go to the center each day and work on writing, or it may be one of a menu of options from which they choose. Children in classrooms with well-stocked and well-organized writing centers often get a lot of experience with writing, too, just as children in writing workshops do. What the writing center doesn't offer children is the support of rigorous *teaching*, or the support you feel when you're surrounded by a whole bunch of others who are learning to do the same thing you're learning to do. While we'll talk a lot more in later chapters about both how we do the teaching and the nature of the curriculum we offer, let's just look here at an overview of when the teaching happens in the workshop.

Each day's sixty- to seventy-five-minute workshop begins with a whole-class lesson that typically lasts from ten to fifteen minutes. These lessons are organized into units of study, series of lessons on some writing topic. One of the most important things to know about these lessons is that they don't give children work to do for the day. The lessons suggest things that children might try or think about as they go about their writing work for the day. The students then go out to work on their writing, to make stuff, and they will be engaged in this for anywhere from thirty-five to fifty minutes. While they are working, we are having individual or small-group conferences with them where we teach

FIGURE 2.2 During share time, Marissa shares a smart writing move.

directly into their specific needs as writers. On a good day, we'll manage to have five or six teaching conferences, affording us the opportunity to meet with each student at least once a week. The workshop ends with a share time that typically lasts about ten minutes, and during this time we usually teach again, sharing specific smart things students have tried in their writing, things that have the potential to raise the level of everyone's work in the room.

Because we believe so strongly in the need to teach students about writing, and because we believe that there can be lots of wonderful depth to the curriculum we offer our youngest writers, we have found that the workshop format works best to help us live out these beliefs with the children we teach.

Getting Started
Understanding the Work

Typically, writing workshop in Lisa's room doesn't actually begin on the very first day or two of school. These are often half-days and she uses them to teach students about the room and to walk them through how everything works and how their days are going to go. She also wants a couple of days to build up their enthusiasm for this thing called writing workshop that they're going to do every day. Usually, a day is set, three of four days into the year, when they will actually begin the workshop, and they spend those first days living toward that launching day.

Several important ideas need to be addressed during these preliminary days before the workshop begins. First, the children need to understand that writing workshop is going to be what they do every day from nine to ten o'clock. It gets explained in the same way that coming in from the buses, going to lunch, recess, reading workshop, and all the other routines of the day get explained. They won't have to wonder what they'll be doing at nine each morning. They'll know—nine o'clock is writing workshop time.

Next, they need a general sense of what writing workshop time is for, what they will be doing during this time every day. This is where they are first introduced to the idea "We're going to make books." Lisa points out published books from their class library that she thinks they might be familiar with, books by Eric Carle especially because she knows and loves his work so well, and she tells the children, "We're going to make books just like Eric does." In doing so she has introduced them right away, before they've even started writing, to the idea that they will learn from authors this year. She likes to show them her Eric Carle video right away, too, because in it Eric talks about beginning his writing career—in kindergarten!

The other thing that is really, really important in helping them understand this work is to show them lots of writing that children like them have done in the past. Lisa tries to represent a wide range of what she expects the new students will be able to do with writing in kindergarten and first grade. She wants all the children to see at least one piece of writing that makes them say, "Hey, I think I could do something like that." So she shares with them pieces that range from fairly crude drawings and no real print all the way up to pieces of writing that have illustrations and fairly sophisticated written texts in them (in the handwriting and spelling of five- and six-year-olds). It is important that she shares both in a way that shows the children she honors them both as writing. So, she talks and talks about the pieces with no real print in them as she goes through them, helping the children see that these books carry meaning and can be read too.

In addition to just looking at the books other children have done in the past, Lisa and her students also talk a lot about what these books are about and how these topics came from the things the children knew about and were interested in. Right away Lisa uses this talk to begin helping her new students think about what they might write about when they start making books of their own. She uses this talk to help them see they are all just full of ideas that could become writing ideas. She also watches the children very closely and listens to them very intently in those early days, knowing that she can learn a lot about their interests if she just pays close attention to them. She will use this knowledge to nudge them into talk that gets their ideas for writing spinning.

Once students do begin writing, the first unit of study—The Kinds of Things Writers Make and How We'll Make Them in This Room— will really be a continuation of these early conversations from the first few days of school. But before children even start, they need some talk about what writing workshop will be (a time for writing every day) and what they'll be doing during that time (making writing stuff).

Understanding Space

The other big idea that is introduced before the workshop begins is how everything will work in the room during the hour-long block of time. We don't want to overwhelm the children with too much information about this; we can expand the range of possibilities as we go. But we do want them to know enough to get started making stuff like the stuff we've been showing them other children have made.

To help them understand enough to get started, Lisa typically does a walk-through to show the children how their workshop will go. She starts them out on the carpet, the class gathering spot, and explains that they will begin each workshop here with a daily lesson about writing. She tells them some of the kinds of things she'll be teaching in these lessons—how to get ideas from books so they can make their own books really neat, different kinds of writing they can try, different things they can do with punctuation, smart ways to come up with spellings for the words they know, and lots more. She explains that she'll do most of the talking in these lessons and that they'll need to listen carefully and always think about their own writing while she's talking. She tells them they need always to be thinking, "Is this something I could try in my writing?"—a question that will end almost every minilesson throughout the year.

Next, she shares whatever management tool she has decided to use to dismiss them from the whole-class lesson and have them go get their supplies and get busy. Typically, she does this by gender and they take turns: girls go first one day, then boys the next.

When dismissed from the whole-class minilesson, the children's first stop will be one of two places: the new paper supply or their writing folders. If they are beginning a new piece of writing, they will need to go and get new paper to get started. There are several choices for size, color, and layout (some lined, some unlined), and at the beginning of the year all of it is stapled together into separate little books (usually with four to six spreads inside). A few weeks into the year, when the idea of bookmaking is clear, Lisa will tell the children they are ready for paper clips if they'd like to use them, instead of prestapled books, and blank paper for this will become another option in the paper sup-

FIGURE 2.3 Lisa begins a morning minilesson.

ply area. After all, the number of pages in a book ultimately should be determined by its content. The paper is kept in a single location in Lisa's room (though you could have more than one location for it if you have a large class), and the children who need it form a line to wait for their turn to choose.

The other first-stop place for children heading out to work is the writing folder bin. If a child is continuing work on a book that's already started, this book will be found in his or her writing folder. In Lisa's room the writing folders are kept in two separate large bins, one for girls and one for boys. There is some physical distance between these two bins so that when the lines form around them at the beginning and end of each workshop, there won't be such a crowd at either of them. After the first day of workshop, when everyone needs new paper to get started, most mornings there is a good mix of children beginning with new paper and those continuing work on an existing piece. They also are told that if they need paper supplies to start a new book or add on to the one they are making during the writing workshop, they should come up and get these on their own.

After Lisa has shown them how to get their paper, she then shows them all the different places in the room they can choose to work. There are no desks in the room, but there are several large tables with chairs, several open and carpeted spots on the floor, and one wonderfully frumpy couch. Children are told they may choose a place somewhere in the room where they think they can work best on their writing. There

FIGURE 2.4 Girls getting their writing work for the morning workshop.

are a few clipboards available for those who might choose not to sit at tables, and Lisa shows them where these are stored so they can get them if they need them. Lisa wants the children to spread out all around the room, as this helps spread out the very natural hum of noise that surrounds young writers at work.

Supplies for writing and making books—cups full of pens, pencils, markers, and crayons; scissors; tape; glue sticks; staplers and staple removers; sticky notes—are located in various places throughout the

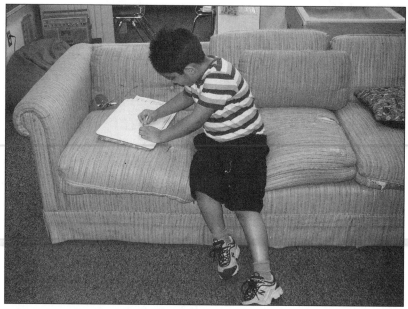

FIGURE 2.5 Cele chooses to work on the couch. Note the cup of pencils and markers he's brought with him.

room so that most of the basic supplies are close at hand no matter where you are working. If something isn't close by and they need it during the workshop, the children are to go and get it on their own.

Understanding Time

Finally, Lisa shows the children the kitchen timer that sits in the middle of the room on top of a file cabinet and helps them manage time during the workshop. She explains to them that she will set it once everyone is settled and working at the beginning of the workshop, and that they are to continue working on making their books each day until they hear the timer ring. She also shows them how they can look at the arrow on the timer and see how far it has to go before the timer will ring, in case they need to check it while they're working. They usually set it for just a single minute the first time and wait for it to go off so they can see how it works.

With the close look at the kitchen timer, and with its prominent position in the center of the classroom in the center of all their work, Lisa helps the children understand right from the start that writing workshop is a time that they will fill up with ongoing activity—making books—not an activity that they will finish. We find that this understanding is very important to helping them manage their work during the workshop. She explains that if they do feel they have finished working on something and the time is not up, then they'll need to find something else to work on until the timer goes off.

On the actual first day of writing workshop, Lisa sets the timer for about fifteen minutes only. She wants them to feel that the time flies by and to feel successful at working for the whole time. She also knows that it will take them a couple of days to become really engaged in something they are making. For the first two weeks or so, then, she gradually increases the amount of time until they are working thirty-five or forty-five minutes a day on their writing and understand that they are to manage their work by time rather than by task.

When the children hear the timer go off each day, Lisa explains that they'll have about five more minutes to find a good stopping place, get their books in progress put back in their folders (in the bins) and their supplies put away, and return to the carpeted meeting area for share time. The little five-minute window of time to do all this keeps everyone from going at once to put things away. Children who have been asked to share some smart thing they've tried during share time are told to bring their work with them to the meeting area instead of putting it away.

At the end of this walk-through that shows the children how everything will work and what they are supposed to do, Lisa explains what she'll be doing—having individual writing conferences with them—while they are working on making their books. At first, she tells them simply that a writing conference is when she will meet with different individuals each day to talk about their writing. She knows that in a few weeks, after they've experienced conferences, they will understand them much better. Lisa explains that the children need to carry on with their work and not interrupt her while she is having writing conferences, but she knows they'll need to be reminded of this a lot in the first weeks of school.

Before the children have ever actually started in their own writing workshop, Lisa has spent time helping them understand exactly how that time will go each day. She wants them to be able to almost picture themselves doing it. She knows that at the beginning there will be lots of reminders of how things work, but the consistent, day-to-day doing of it in the exact same way will help it become routine fairly quickly. And because establishing the routine is so important, she is careful not to do anything to throw it off in those first weeks of school. She wants it to become just the way we do things in this class in the students' minds.

Establishing Guidelines

Typically, after the writing workshop has been up and going for about two weeks, Lisa finds it helpful to review the whole process of it with the children. At this time, one or two mornings' minilessons will be spent going over the procedures and troubleshooting any problems Lisa has identified at this point. During these minilessons, the class will establish their first written guidelines (on a large chart) for the workshop. The specifics of the guidelines may vary a little in wording and in content from year to year depending on the students' needs. During one school year, the chart had these things listed on it:

- Get your tools ready—pencils, crayons, markers, erasers, paper, writing from your writing folders.
- Find the best place for you to work—around friends who won't distract you.
- You may talk—asking a friend for help, sharing ideas. . . .
- Write until the bell goes off on the timer.

- Stay in the place you have chosen to write. Don't get up unless you are looking for an idea, need more tools, or need to go to the word wall or to find a book.

- When the bell goes off, you have five more minutes to find a good stopping place, clean up, and meet at group time.

- Be ready to listen!

As you might imagine, there are often times when the chart needs to be revisited for one reason or another during the year. There may also be guidelines that need to be added along the way for the whole class, or we may find the need to make specific guidelines that apply only to specific children who have problems with some aspect of the management. We're not afraid to do this and when we do, we simply explain to the children that they need this guideline because they aren't managing some aspect of their work well on their own.

We believe it is important to pay attention to the management of time and space across the year because the two essentials of the workshop—children getting valuable writing experience and our making a place for the teaching of writing—depend on things running as smoothly as possible. To have successful workshops, we all have to make decisions about the management of the time when children are working on their writing. We make these decisions based on the layout and size of our classrooms, the number of students we have, and, to a certain extent, our own teaching styles.

The management in Lisa's workshop described here has evolved and continues to evolve over time in her teaching. We certainly don't believe it is the only management system that can be effective; we simply shared it to give you one snapshot of a workshop that runs smoothly on most days. As you develop your own management for young children, we know from experience that there are a few essential questions that need to be answered before the workshop begins:

- How will students get from place to place—minilesson to work time to share time?

- Where in the room will students be allowed to work on their writing? Will they work in the same place each day, or will they decide this each day?

- Where will the supplies for writing and their ongoing work be kept, and how will they get these and put them back each day? How will they get things they need *during* the workshop?

Finished Writing

One of the first management issues we will need to address once the writing workshop is up and running is what it means to be finished with a piece of writing. Through the years, as our thinking has evolved and we have found reasons to start all the children out making books, we have found that at the start we need to talk about being finished as a means to address paper conservancy as much as anything else. In other words, before children get another blank book and start another piece of writing, we need to let them know what we expect to see in the one they are working in currently. This past year, Lisa established these guidelines at the beginning of the year for being finished with a book:

I KNOW I'M FINISHED WHEN . . .

- All of my pages are *full* of writing and illustrations and are about the same big idea.
- All of my illustrations go along with my words.
- I have a date stamp and my name on my book.
- I have shared my writing with someone who would be interested in it.

Now, this is certainly not the deep, writing-process understanding of being finished we hope students will develop over time as writers; it is simply a way to help them stay with a piece of writing longer right from the start and, of course, not to waste paper. You may notice that the guidelines also communicate some fairly important understandings about composing a written text: that it should all be about one idea and that everything in the text should relate to that one idea.

Essentially, every child who enters writing workshop can successfully follow these guidelines to finish writing right from the start, especially since we have shown them what we consider to be writing across a wide range of developmental levels. We also understand that most of them won't start out doing these things very well, especially sticking to the big idea and making the illustrations match the words (for those who have words), but that's OK. Our later teaching is for helping them do these things better and better. At the start we just want them making the best attempts they can to do these things and to come to some under-standing of what it means to be finished. When we feel like they do understand this, then we will go ahead and let them start some new pieces before others are finished, helping them see that they can come back and work more on something (left unfinished) later.

As the year progresses and the children get more writing experi-ence and we do lots of teaching to support new understandings, we may add guidelines for being finished. We might add things such as

- I can read all the words I've written.
- I can tell you the genre of my piece.
- I have used punctuation in my piece (and can explain how I've used it).
- I have tried to craft my writing (and can explain how I did it).
- I have reread my piece and am sure I've made it as good as it can be.
- I have reread my piece and am sure there are no words left out.
- I have edited my piece for high-frequency spellings I should know.

Guidelines such as these may be written on a class chart or be printed as little checksheets students fill out when they finish something. Either way, they'll need to be supported with lots of talk about what they mean. We'll also want to watch for children who follow these guidelines well and be sure to share what they are doing with the other students.

With any guidelines we develop across the year, we need to re-member that some children will not yet be ready to use those guidelines to direct their work. We can use the same guidelines for everyone, but if we do, it needs to be OK for children to approximate this finishing process in developmentally appropriate and different ways. We have to work to maintain a balance between having expectations the children feel they can successfully meet and having expectations that challenge children to do better and better work as writers, and we have to do this while thinking about children at many different developmental levels.

One of the things we have to decide is what will happen to writing that is finished. Because the depth of their engagement in all aspects of the process is not the same as that of more experienced writers, our youngest writers will finish lots of pieces of writing during the school year. What happens to this writing? We know a number of options for managing finished writing, though one thing is for sure: children should be able to finish and move on to something new without a teacher's intervention. If we don't establish this, we will have too many children sitting around waiting for us after they have finished something. So, what are some options for managing finished work?

We might have a box or basket where children put their pieces of writing when they are finished. If we do, we'll check the box regularly and we'll likely take some of these finished pieces with us to writing conferences so we can talk through the writing with the individual children. We'll also be on the lookout for smart things we see children doing that we want to bring to others' attention during minilessons or share times, and of course we'll use the finished pieces for ongoing assessment of students' work. After we've looked at finished work, we can either give it back to the children to take home or give away to an intended audience, or we can save it (or a copy of it) in another folder—one for each child—of representative writing from across the year.

FIGURE 2.6 Steven gets something out of his ongoing work folder during the workshop.

We might have the children simply put finished pieces of writing in their ongoing work folders. Keeping the writing here gives children the opportunity to go back to something they may have thought was finished, but have decided to revisit, which we find they do fairly often in Lisa's workshop. If we keep finished pieces in the ongoing work folder, then we'll need to be sure to do two things. First, we'll need to check in with the children routinely and ask them to show us finished pieces. We'll want to make sure they are following the guidelines for finishing pieces to the best of their individual abilities, and that writing that has an intended audience is getting into the hands of that audience. Second, we'll need to clean the folders out periodically. Just like anything that is really used by six-year-olds, they will get fairly messy fairly quickly. Again, after a cleaning, we'll need a place to save representative pieces that show growth over time for each child.

Some of the children's writing will likely go into the class library after it is finished (there's usually just too much for all of it to go there), and we'll need to decide on a process for this. One option is to have children choose a piece periodically that they want to go into the library. This is, in some ways, a form of self-assessment, as we ask children to decide, out of all their work, what they'd like to contribute. We may do a little fancier publishing with these books, making more durable covers for them or typing some of them up on the computer and reillustrating them, or we may not. We can just place them as is—in all their joyful messiness—in a certain place in the library for class authors. After all, we certainly want most of these books to actually look like children wrote them.

While we'll ask children to share their writing with someone before considering it finished, and while we'll share selected pieces that have teaching potential during the everyday share time, we may also want to build in time periodically when children choose finished pieces to share with a larger audience, just for the sake of sharing them. We might do this with just our class, or we might do it with another class who also has writing workshop. Once or twice a year, we might invite parents and other interested outsiders to a celebration of sharing from our finished writing.

Writing workshop right from the start. Those early days will matter so much to the success of the workshop across the year. And what a journey it is for us as teachers to keep thinking and rethinking how we launch children into this work. Every year we feel a little bit stronger in our understanding of what we need to do in these early days, and every year when it's all up and going, we make plans for how *next* year will be even better.

CHAPTER 3

Wrapping Strong Arms Around the Writing Workshop

Children Learning About Language All Day Long

Katie will never forget the day she came upon Forrest working on a nonfiction book about sea creatures. She watched him carefully labor over the generation of the text in Figure 3.1. Katie was so curious about the *k* in "sea anemone." "Why did he put a *k* in that word?" she wondered. And then she asked Forrest about it. "You know, like in *knee*," he said. "Sea anemo*ne*."

During word study time in the mornings before writing workshop, Lisa and the children had been working on understanding that what they know about the sound and spelling of one word can help them spell or read an unfamiliar word. They had looked at many, many examples of words where this was true and talked about how they could figure them out. *Sea anemone* was not one of the words the children had looked at during word study, but Forrest used the strategy Lisa had taught him and figured this spelling out all on his own to help him with his writing during writing workshop.

Learning About Language All Day Long

To really understand the writing children do during the hour-long writing workshop, it is important to understand that this is not the only

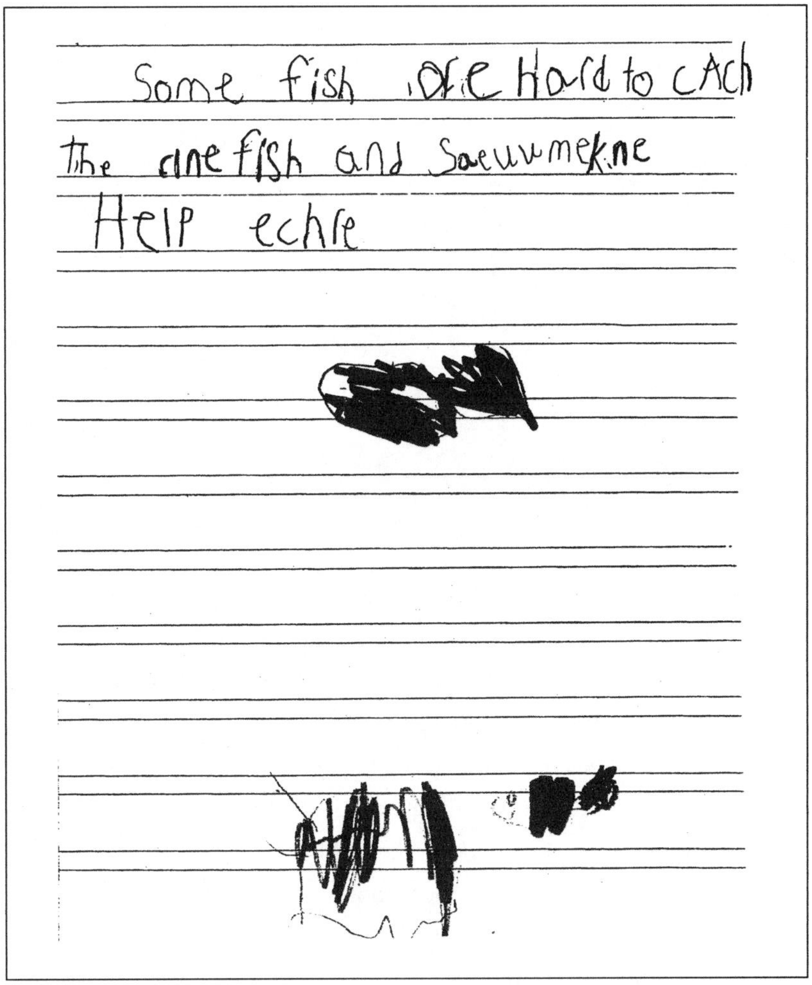

Some fish are Hard to cACh
the cinefish and Saeuvmek.ne
Help echre

FIGURE 3.1 From Forrest's book about sea creatures. Some fish are hard to catch. The clown fish and sea anemone help each other.

time in the day that they are learning about how our language works. Writing workshop is simply a time when children get to try their hands at making written language work—at generating text—all on their own. As you'll see in later chapters, much of the whole-class teaching during writing workshop is about helping children deepen their knowledge of the process and craft of writing used for composition. So how and when do we teach children about the conventions of written language that help them generate text? The answer to this is, literally, all day long. For the writing that children do on their own to be successful, we must wrap strong arms of teaching about how written language works around that hour of workshop each day.

We'll need a rich variety of activities and engagements to help children learn about language all day long. We'll also need to find ways for children to use writing for purposes other than composition throughout the day. Let's look now at a sort of menu of a few different ways we might support children in learning about the conventions of written language outside of writing workshop. We'll consider:

> environmental support
> reading aloud
> talking into our routines
> writing demonstrations
> word study
> center work
> songs and games
> writing to support other work

Now, we certainly didn't invent this kind of work and we assume most who read this book already know a lot about working with children in these ways. The kinds of things we have our students doing to learn the specifics of language use are really not that different from what most primary teachers have their students doing. The difference, of course, is the balance of time and intention. All the language study we plan for students is meant to *support* the writing workshop time each day, where the real writing work happens, not to *become* the writing work itself. Because of that, one thing you'll notice in this menu is that there isn't a lot of whole-class time for practicing various bits and pieces of what writers need to know, not a lot of time spent copying the daily sentence or doing *c* activities for the week or filling in blanks in someone else's story. Basically, we feel that while these kinds of activities might teach children something, they are not teaching them how to write because the children aren't writing when they do them, they're not doing the hard work of *generating text*. These activities often lead to pretty pieces of writing, but we don't see the evidence of deeply engaged thinking we do when children are writing themselves.

As we look at the menu possibilities, we must remember that the ways we'll choose to support any given group of students will depend on what those students already know about how our language works and what we see they still need to know.

Environmental Support

While we know students won't learn all they need to know about how written language works simply by being surrounded by print, we don't underestimate the power of environmental print to support language learning either. The walls, desks, tables, sides of bookcases, even the floors—basically, every flat surface in a primary classroom—can be filled

FIGURE 3.2 The room is rich with environmental print.

with print that children can look at, wonder and talk about, and use as a reference when they need it to help them with their own writing.

Alphabet charts, number charts, color charts, calendars, signs and labels of all sorts, lists of students' names, word walls, class charts, directions and support print for various centers and activities—the room needs to be rich with print resources. We have also found that—especially in kindergarten—it is helpful to have alphabet strips on the actual tables at which children will be working so they can use them

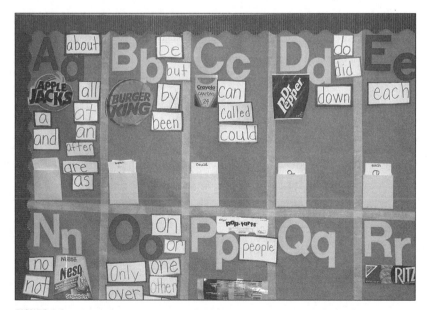

FIGURE 3.3 An alphabet chart with high-frequency words and environmental print.

easily if they need reminders of how the letters are formed. From time to time we can talk about the various print in the room to make sure students are utilizing it as they learn about and use written language. We'll also need all sorts of written texts in the room to give students visions of different kinds of published writing—picture books, obviously, but also newspapers, magazines, charts with poems and songs written on them, reference books, and more.

Reading Aloud

Every time we read aloud to children, for whatever reason, we are teaching writing. How else would children know what good writing is supposed to *sound* like if we didn't read aloud to them? We are very careful to read aloud well, minding the craft of the writing as well as the meaning. For example, if there is a particularly strong word choice or some artful repetition, we are sure to read it so the children can really hear how the language is working. We want our read-alouds to tune their ears to the sound of writing when it's right and to expose children to rich language and more sophisticated texts than they are able to read on their own. And when they read a piece of their writing, we encourage them to read it as if it were a read-aloud book and we listen to hear if they are honoring their own texts as literature. We know that learning to hear how a text sounds will grow to be one of the most important revision tools they will use as more experienced writers.

Talking into Our Routines

Martha Gregory, a fellow teacher of our youngest writers, can work a lunch menu into a phonics and spelling lesson like nobody's business. Each day as her young students look at what's for lunch and think about what selections they'll make, Martha uses the words they see there to create a language lesson for the day. Going over the lunch menu is routine, predictable, and provides a lot repetition of words to scaffold their learning.

Like Martha, many teachers look to the routines of the day as language-learning opportunities. "If the name of your favorite ice cream starts with a *v*, you can get in line now. . . ," or "Let's spell *home* together before we go get our things ready to go home today," or "Look for a word you haven't noticed before as we walk along and go to lunch today," or "Oh look, this bag I brought the rocks in says *Wal-Mart*." It's so easy to do this teaching if we just remember that we need to do it. The opportunities for it are endless.

When we embed talk about language into our routines of the day, we really help our young students become people who just love to talk about language and are fascinated by how it all works. Interestingly, most of the students who come to school already knowing a lot about how

FIGURE 3.4 Katie writes in front of the students.

written language works have had someone embedding talk about language for years into the routines of their days at home.

Writing Demonstrations

There are multiple opportunities in any given day in a primary classroom for the teacher to write in front of students—writing morning or afternoon news or announcements, for example, recording students' observations or responses during content area discussions, composing language experience stories from something the class has done together, or writing out the steps to some class procedure. Most teachers use these opportunities to embed teaching about the conventions of written language. As they write in front of the class, they draw students' attention to specific language information. Depending on the kinds of language information children need, teachers may highlight letter names and letter formation, sounds that different letters make, spellings and spelling patterns, spacing between words, capitalization and punctuation, sentence structure, or the kinds of thinking a writer does as text is generated. Sometimes teachers have students interact with this writing and help them generate the text in these demonstrations.

Word Study

In many primary classrooms there is some time for focused word study each day. In Lisa's room, word study often happens just before the writing workshop minilesson. The word study is direct and systematic and ranges from beginning-of-the-year work with letters and sounds to studies of phonics, spelling patterns, word families, syllabication, and so forth. The

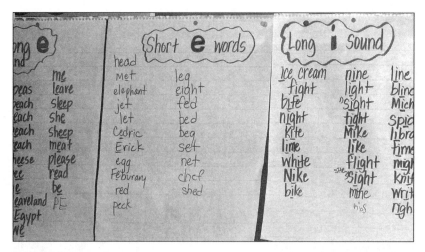

FIGURE 3.5 Charts from word study.

FIGURE 3.6 Charts from word study.

talk during word study moves seamlessly between how the information helps children with their reading and how it helps with their writing. Sometimes children are asked to complete some written work, either as part of the word study time or later in the day, that is meant to support the study. Sometimes, the deep talk and thinking around word study is simply meant to follow them into writing and reading workshop.

Related to this, some primary teachers have first graders work at committing the spellings of a small number of high-frequency words to memory each week. Sometimes there is one list for the whole class, and sometimes the lists are individualized. Either way, when students are responsible for such a list, there is usually some repetitious spelling of the required words during each day of the week they are under study. This spelling work is always better work if we design it so that children have to think about how the word is spelled each time they generate it

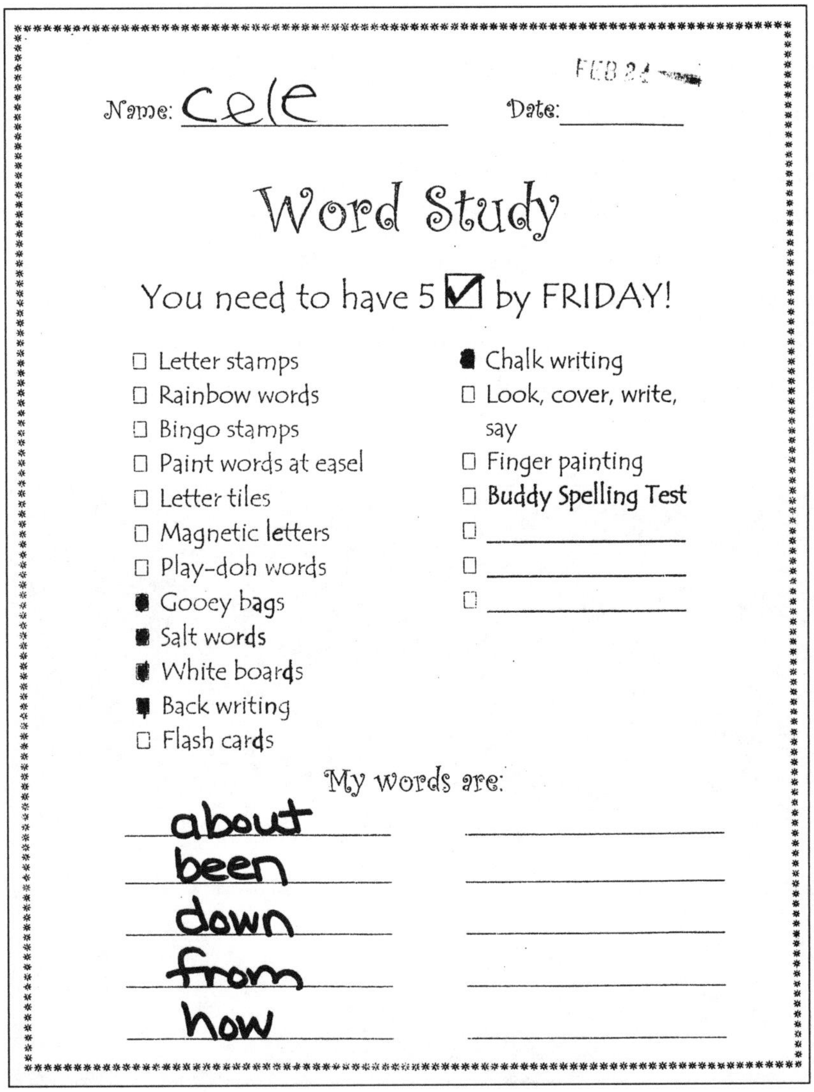

Name: Cele   Date: _____   FEB 24

Word Study

You need to have 5 ☑ by FRIDAY!

- ☐ Letter stamps
- ☐ Rainbow words
- ☐ Bingo stamps
- ☐ Paint words at easel
- ☐ Letter tiles
- ☐ Magnetic letters
- ☐ Play-doh words
- ☑ Gooey bags
- ☑ Salt words
- ☑ White boards
- ☑ Back writing
- ☐ Flash cards

- ☑ Chalk writing
- ☐ Look, cover, write, say
- ☐ Finger painting
- ☐ **Buddy Spelling Test**
- ☐ _____
- ☐ _____
- ☐ _____

My words are:

about   _____
been   _____
down   _____
from   _____
how   _____

FIGURE 3.7 A student's sheet showing his choices of word study for one week in February.

(copying doesn't require thinking about how it's spelled). This spelling practice takes place outside of writing workshop.

We should note that we understand why many of the words children work on with spelling practice don't come out spelled conventionally in their writing work. When children are only spelling, all they have to think about is spelling. When they are spelling as a part of generating text, there are so many other things they have to be thinking about at the same time as they are spelling. We do believe, however, that some specific spelling work can help children begin to reread their written texts with an eye for editing the spelling of high-frequency words.

Center Work

Many primary classrooms have centers that students visit during the day, and often one or more of these centers has some kind of language study embedded in the work of the center. Students may be using magnetic letters to make words and messages on metal tablets, manipulating stamps and stickers with letters and words on them, cutting out environmental print from newspapers and labels, or practicing different letter formations and handwriting.

Songs and Games

Many teachers sing songs and play games that teach students about how written language works. Singing is such a joyful engagement with young children. There is the classic alphabet song, of course, but there are others that help students remember spellings and letter sounds as well. Lisa's university intern, Emily, with all her background in performance and

FIGURE 3.8 A center with stamps.

FIGURE 3.9 Games that help children learn about language.

theatre, was wonderful at using songs to support the lessons she taught during word study time in the mornings: "*A* has two sounds, *a* has two sounds, *a* as in *Taylor*, *a* as in *Ashley*, *a* and *a*, *a* and *a*" (to the tune of "Are You Sleeping?"). We can also think of games that teach language concepts and play them from time to time or have them available for children to play on their own—beginners' versions of Scrabble® and hangman, for example.

Writing to Support Other Work

Most primary teachers are careful to make sure that students are writing to support other content areas and activities during the day. This other writing does the dual work of teaching them about the conventions of written language and helping them explore other functions of writing. A lot of this will be writing students do all on their own (in the sense that they generate the text by themselves), just as the work they do in writing workshop. Here's a short list of some kinds of writing students might do on their own:

- observations of things
- reading responses
- logs that document work for the day in different content areas
- explanations for problem solving in math or science
- notes to the teacher or other students

- writing to support creative play—taking orders in a restaurant center, making a grocery list in a housekeeping center, writing labels or signs for structures built with blocks and Legos™, and so on

- signing up, signing in, and signing out—attendance, lunch choices, center choices, book choices, and so on

Some of this writing during the day may be scaffolded, as with students filling in a word or phrase in an already written text. This requires them to use the skills of reading comprehension as well. And some teachers find opportunities for students to copy writing down from time to time—homework assignments, lists of things to do, names of children in their group, titles of books they read, and so forth. Now, copying is not the same thing as writing. Not at all. A person who is copying something isn't generating text and doesn't have to think of all those complex things at once that a person who is writing has to think about. The value (in terms of learning to write) in copying something that's already written is probably in the service of handwriting and letter formation only, as it provides a model of exactly what the writing should look like right there as you are forming the letters and words on the page (as we said earlier, copying doesn't require any thinking about spelling). Certainly, if good handwriting is something a teacher values a lot, then children will likely do more copying to support that goal.

So there we have it—a menu of kinds of things we can plan to support children in learning the conventions of language. And of course, we didn't even consider that children will be spending extended periods of time during the day reading and that every time they read (or are read to), they are learning about how written language works as well. Whatever we plan for our individual classrooms, the key is to have children step into writing workshop each day out of an environment just saturated with talking and thinking about language and how it works.

But Where, Exactly, Do We Start?

The explanation that there is so much language learning supporting the daily writing workshop makes a lot of sense to almost anyone trying to understand this teaching. Even so, we are often asked, "But how do you start writing workshop when they haven't even learned to write yet? Wouldn't there need to be some beginning understandings about language in place before the children could actually begin writing? Wouldn't writing be a lot *easier* for children if they knew more about it before you asked them to start making books?"

Often, it's parents who want to know the answers to these good questions, and we can't ask them to please just read a little Brian Cambourne and Frank Smith, a little Sandra Wilde and Lev Vygotsky so they'll understand what we're doing with their children. We can't ask them to do the homework we've done to come to understand this teaching. We need clear, articulate explanations for why we're doing the work we're doing that will make sense to parents (and any other interested constituents), but more importantly, that will make sense to us as teachers in practical, day-to-day ways. So, how do we start writing workshop when they haven't even learned to write yet? Let's think that through next.

Understanding *Writing* as a Noun and a Verb

First of all, we do not believe that learning to write begins in some moment of time, with some first thing, some beginning place that we can mark and then do first in kindergarten. We don't believe that learning to write begins, for example, with learning to make the letter *a*. We believe that when children first come to school, they have already started learning to write. All of them have started learning, no matter their background experiences, because all of them come to us knowing something about written language, even if it's just that it *exists*. They know this because they've lived for five years in a world surrounded by the symbols of print, some more surrounded than others, for sure, but all of them have seen lots of print, even if they've never tried to make any of these symbols themselves or seen many others try to make them.

Because we believe they come to school already on their way to learning to write, the first thing we want to do is get writing tools in their hands, paper in front of them, and see what they know when they get there. And here's the thing: we call whatever they do with those tools and that paper *writing*. *That's* how we start writing workshop when they haven't even learned to write yet. Now, in doing this, we think about the fact that the word *writing* can be used as both a verb (to write) and a noun. It's *writing* as a verb that what we are asking them to do at the beginning of writing workshop. The very first definition listed for the verb *write* in Webster's Collegiate dictionary reads like this: "to form (as characters or symbols) on a surface with an instrument (as a pen)." Any five-year-old who can physically hold a writing tool in hand can do that!

Now, the writing they produce is writing in the noun sense of the word, as in "something written." The characters and symbols we see they've formed on a surface with an instrument may not be ones we recognize, they may not look at all like something written by an adult, but that doesn't mean the children weren't writing when they produced them. The very first books written at the beginning of the year by kindergartners are going to look like five-year-olds wrote them all by themselves. In essence, then, to get children started writing in the verb sense, we have to accept that their writing in the noun sense is going to look like it was done by five-year-olds.

Sometimes we wonder, "Don't I at least need to teach them how to make each of the letters of the alphabet before they start to write?" But then we need to ask ourselves, "What, exactly, is there to *teach* about this?" Children don't really need any *information* about how to make a *b* other than what it looks like. Basically they have to get markers in their hands and use what fine motor control they have to make something that looks like that *b* they've seen thousands of times in their lives and is probably on an alphabet chart somewhere very near them at that moment. Basically, they just start out drawing a *b* in much the same way they start out drawing flowers and suns and rainbows, which we never teach them how to draw either, by the way. They've seen them, they've seen others make them, and they follow along.

Children can and will begin forming letters in their writing before they even know what those letters are called and certainly before they know what sounds they all make. We get those writing tools in their hands, surround them with print so they are constantly reminded what letters look like, and then, as we explained earlier in this chapter, we immerse them in looking at what those letters do to form words, what sounds they can make, and how they can join with others to make new sounds. We also watch them very closely as we work side by side in conferring and help them with any particular issues we see related to letter formation or handwriting.

Of course, it is easy for us to say as their teachers that we'll get them writing right away, but what if the children themselves don't believe they can write because they haven't even learned to write yet? We don't really give them a chance to think they can't write; to get them started, we tell them just to pretend to write if they'd like. Now, we don't really believe they are pretending. We believe they are writing, as defined earlier, and that every moment they spend doing that is a moment that *matters* on their journey to learning to write well. We just know that pretending is something all children believe they can do, so we use this word if we need to use it to help get them started.

Some of them have to pretend more than others.

They come to us in kindergarten representing a continuum between two extremes. On one end of the continuum are children who have obviously had very little experience with paper and writing tools.

These children may not be quite sure how to hold the pencil or marker or even which end should connect with the paper, but they watch what the others around them do and figure it out and, somewhat awkwardly, they follow along when it's time to write. For these children, it will be a while before they'll have any words to reread in their writing. This is one extreme.

On the other extreme, we have children who come to us in kindergarten already writing a small repertoire of words and they have some tools to generate other words, meaning they already know some (or all) of the letters and the sounds they make. These children started "pretending" to write some time ago, and they had someone talking to them about writing along the way. And then we have everything, developmentally speaking, in between these two extremes.

By first grade, a year of kindergarten has eliminated the most extreme left side of the continuum for many children—many of them will have had experience with writing tools and paper, but we still see a broad range of development in writing, just as we do with all academic, physical, and social development. Often, the *kinds* of experiences children had with writing in kindergarten vary a lot in a single first-grade classroom, and this has a huge influence on what we see they are able to do at the beginning of the year. Children who mostly copied writing in kindergarten, for example, have had very little experience generating text on their own. They'll need lots of support at first in knowing how to come up with good spellings for words they want to write.

We still smile when we think about Sarah, a fabulous teaching intern with Lisa a few years back. Near the end of the year, Sarah found out she had been offered a job teaching the next year in a K–2 classroom. She was anxious about it, not sure if she could do it because she had never taught all those developmental levels at once. "Yes, you have," we told her. "You've been teaching first grade." Even when teaching in a "straight" first-grade classroom, we see a very wide range of development across the day in children's various engagements, and especially with writing.

Why Keep Them Writing When They Don't Know Much About It?

We spend the first few days of writing workshop in both kindergarten and first grade watching to see what knowledge of the conventions of written language children bring with them. But we also want to see what they know about what writing is for and what it can do in the world. Do they have a sense that what they write should sound like some kind of thing they have read (or has been read to them)? We have to get them started writing right away to know what they know. But what happens if we look closely in those first few days and we see that they don't know much about written language at all? Why would we spend so much time to keep them writing and pretending to write every day when they still need to know so much?

Writing Shows Us What They Are Learning About Writing

As we said in the beginning of this chapter, writing workshop is not the only time when children are learning about written language and how it all works. For the workshop to be successful, children need to be talking about language, manipulating language, playing with language, using language purposefully, and watching demonstrations of adults using language all day long. But the thing is, to see if all our language teaching is making any difference in their learning to write, we have to let them write! While we might be interested in seeing that they know what sound *t* makes or how to make a perfect letter *g* or that they can edit the sentence of the day on our chart paper, at some point we need to know whether any of that language work is making a difference. Is it really teaching them *how to write*? How would we know this if they didn't have time to write each day? To put it simply, one reason we keep them writing is because we need to see if they are learning to write from all our teaching.

Writing Is Generating Text

We also keep them writing because we believe they actually have to do it in order to learn to do it. There is absolutely no substitute, nothing you can practice or simulate, that teaches you to do the thinking necessary to *generate text* other than trying your hand at it. When someone actually writes, he has to bring together layers and layers of many separate pieces of information to generate the text that helps him say what he wants to say. And while we will teach and teach them all about this information, we also want them to learn to bring that information together and get experience generating text. The bits and pieces need to add up to something. Forrest, for example, needs a chance to *use* the information from word study that knowledge of one word can help him spell another word, as he did with *sea anemone*.

When we watch young children generate text on their own, we realize what an incredible intellectual challenge it is, and we watch them rise to meet this challenge again and again. Think of all the things they have to think about just to get an idea down. These things are so automatic for us, but beginners have to think very specifically about what they want to say, what words they'll need to say it, what order the words should go in, which letters they need to write each word, how to form each of those letters, where the spaces go, where the punctuation might go, and on and on. And they have to do all this while they are still holding the big idea in their heads. It's deeply intellectual work we ask them to do when we ask them to write on their own. To put it simply, children need time to write so they can use all the separate bits and pieces of information about written language we are giving them to actually generate text.

Writing Is About More Than Just Conventions

We also keep them writing because we want them to learn more about writing than just the conventions of it. We want them to learn about the wonderful potentials of different genres and the promise of crafting techniques that help writers write well. We want them to learn about the process of writing and what it's like to live a writing life every day where they use that process to write their own books. Think back to Josh's piece about mammoths in the opening chapter of this book. Remember the list of all the things he knows about writing that we can see in that single text? He knows all those things because he has been deeply engaged in exploring writing in all these ways, all year. He's been making books during writing workshop from day one, and he's used writing across the day to serve all sorts of other purposes. He has developed all the essential understandings of the conventions of language that we expect a first grader to develop, but he has learned so much more about writing in addition to this.

From experience, we have come to see again and again that children can learn about the craft and process of writing at the same time as they are learning about the conventions of writing. It's not a chicken-and-egg question, after all. Defining *writing* as a verb means they can start writing right away. We see so many children who spend years in school waiting to really explore the craft and process of writing in different genres, waiting to learn all those things Josh and his classmates know at the end of first grade about making a piece of literature, waiting because someone thinks they *still* don't know enough about spelling and punctuation and how to form a good sentence or paragraph to move on to those other things. We just don't believe in making children wait to learn about the craft and process of writing.

Taylor, for example, is a child who might have been made to wait on writing if we thought it was necessary to have all the "prerequisites" in place first. Figure 3.10 shows a writing sample from him in the early days of the writing workshop.

FIGURE 3.10 Taylor's early writing. The words were copied from the card center. He wasn't confident that he could write on his own when he started.

But Taylor wasn't made to wait, and by the end of the year he showed us once again why we have so much faith in children and in the work we ask them to do in the writing workshop. Figure 3.11 shows a piece of Taylor's writing from the end of the year. Look at all he's learned.

Writing has become an important part of how Taylor responds to the world, and he's learned lots about the conventions of writing in the process.

FIGURE 3.11 In May, Taylor wrote *The Book About Fish* on the bus on the way back from a class trip to an aquarium. (1) The book about fish. (2) This is an octopus. (3) This is a sea snake. (4) This is a jelly fish.

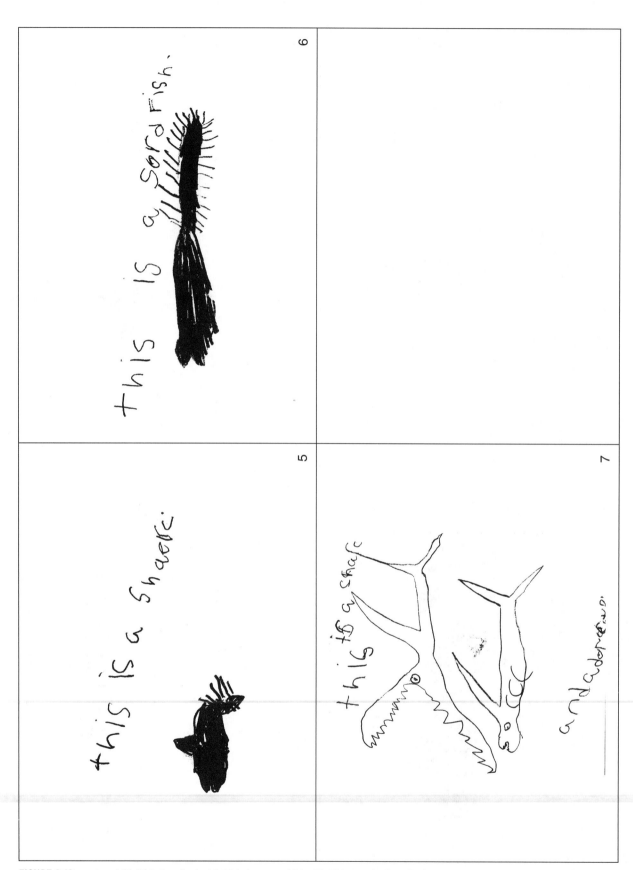

FIGURE 3.12 *continued* (5) This is a shark. (6) This is a swordfish. (7) This is a shark and a barracuda.

We also recognize that in teaching young children lots about the craft and process of writing as we teach them about the conventions of writing, we are increasing the likelihood that they will be able to use writing successfully in the lives they find for themselves someday. We know that the bottom line is our students need a solid knowledge of conventions to be able to write successfully. However, we also know that they will never be successful writers if that is *all* they have. There is so much more involved in writing well than just good proofreading skills.

People aren't getting letters to the editor or professional journal articles or short stories published because all their words are spelled correctly and all their commas are in the right place. They aren't getting into great colleges or landing the jobs they want because their letters of application have fabulous handwriting in them and wonderfully chunked paragraphs. When writing is successful, it has to be about more than that. Good writing comes from having a compelling idea and then knowing how to shape that idea with form and genre and structure and write about it clearly with voice and style. Good writing requires you to find a process that helps you stay with it until it's finished. We believe it will take years of experience using this process for our students to become the successful writers we envision them to be, and we don't want to put that experience off for even a moment. We especially don't want to put it off when they have shown us again and again that they are so ready to begin thinking about it right from the start when they make their very first books.

Writing Well Is Something We Know How to Teach Students to Do

Finally, we want to keep students writing because we have learned that there is so much to teach them. For years as teachers of writing, we could get away with teaching only conventions because that was pretty much all we knew to teach about writing. Many of us thought that the rest of what a writer was able to do was just talent or giftedness. But we realize now that this just isn't true. There is a whole body of knowledge out there about how writers learn about genre, structure, and the craft of writing, as well as so much information about how writers engage in the process of writing. We believe that it's not OK for us to act as if we are teaching all there is to teach if we focus only on the conventions of writing. We can't in good conscience know what we now know about writing and about children's language development and still spend all our time teaching them to make beautiful letter *m*s. There is just so much more for us to offer our students.

4

How Our Youngest Writers Use the Writing Process to Help Them Make Books

One morning before writing workshop begins, we overhear Cauley explaining to one of his classmates an idea he has for the book he's working on at the time. The book is about snakes, and Cauley says, "I was thinking last night that in my book, if the snake makes a mistake, I could call it a *missnake*. Get it, a mis*snake*?" We smile, both at Cauley's wonderful way with language and at the evidence that he's using the writing process just as a much more experienced writer would use it: he's thinking about what he's working on when he's not actually at his desk engaged in writing it.

Ever since Donald Graves and his colleagues first pushed many of us in the early eighties to look closely at what experienced writers do when they write, the study of writing as a process has been informing the teaching of writing in significant ways. Over the years, we've continued to look to experienced writers as we've explored what it means to choose ideas, prewrite, draft, revise, edit, and publish writing, and we've deepened our understandings about this very complex, recursive process in so many ways. And as teachers of our youngest writers, we find ourselves constantly trying to understand what this process looks like when these very inexperienced writers use it and, perhaps even more challeng-

FIGURE 4.1 Cauley creates a spelling for the play-on-word he's created.

ing, trying to figure out what we should teach about process that makes sense in the context of a six-year-old's work.

In this chapter we want to share some of what we've learned about what the writing process looks like when our youngest writers use it. The teaching that we do during the year to help them refine this process—which we'll discuss in later chapters—must begin with our understanding how they use it. Before we walk through the process itself, though, a few big ideas seem worth noting.

First, we should make it clear that we don't teach students the process before we have them begin writing. We don't even quickly name the steps of it before they start; we probably wouldn't do this at any grade level, actually. Instead, we would begin a writing workshop by handing out the paper and the writing tools and asking students just to get started and go ahead and make something with writing. We expect them to use whatever process they are able to use to get that done. Once they are up and writing, then we'll begin to watch them very closely and teach into what we see them doing (and not doing), helping them refine all the ways they go about writing—from ideas to finished pieces.

We do this because we know that the process as we know it didn't exist *before* people were writing. We came to understand the process of writing because people were already writing. We watched what they did and named it as a process. But the process existed *before* anyone named it, and it makes instructional sense to us that it should exist in our classrooms before we begin teaching about it. We want students to be engaged in using some process (after all, you can't make a book without using *some* sort of process), trying their best to make a piece of writing, and then our teaching should help them refine what they are already doing to get writing finished.

Related to this, while we know that all writers find ideas, prewrite, draft, revise, edit, and publish, we also know that there are lots of different ways that writers go about using this process effectively. There is not some set list of steps or things to do that always works for every writer on every piece of writing. Essentially, the goal (again, at any grade level) is for writers to find a process that helps them go from an idea to the best piece of finished writing they can possibly produce, not for them to jump through management hoops we've set up in the name of process. This is why we believe we need to see how they are going about getting their writing done first, then the teaching of process involves suggesting options they might try to help them do it better.

Approaching the teaching of process in this way perhaps feels a little less organized than if we had procedures for them to follow for each step of the process, but we feel like it more closely matches what writers actually do. We believe students need to get in there and muck about inside the process to find ways of working that are right for them.

Finally, it's important that we understand that the process is one writers use for *composition*. We use writing for lots of reasons in our lives, and especially in our learning lives—to fill things out, jot things down, give answers, reflect on ideas. We want children to use writing for a variety of these purposes every day in school. But writing used in this way is not the same as writing used to compose. It's a whole lot easier, for one thing, and it doesn't involve the complex process that writing as composition does. In *The Writing Workshop: Working Through the Hard Parts (and They're All Hard Parts)* (Ray with Laminack 2001), Katie defines composition in this way:

> Writing as composition is writing that begins with an idea a writer
> wants to communicate. The idea is developed in the writer's think-
> ing, and then, at some point, the move toward composition is
> made. This move is the beginning move toward an audience, to-
> ward readers. This move means that the writer will now have to
> take this idea he or she has developed and begin to shape it with

genre, form, sound, and the conventions of the language system all working together to produce a piece that has the desired impact on readers. This move begins the very complex act of writing as composition. (19)

Children in classrooms where writing is mixed in with everything else often aren't getting much experience with the actual process of composition, because most of the mixed-in writing doesn't require it. Writing workshop is a place where we want children learning to use a process to compose writing for an audience, reason again to start them all out making picture books, the kind of composition most familiar to them.

So let's look closely now at the different aspects of the process of writing as it is used by our youngest writers. As we go along, we'll keep in mind the understandings we have about process from our studies of what professional writers say and from our own experiences with writing. We need these understandings because they give direction and vision to our teaching. We don't expect six-year-olds to engage in the process as experienced writers do, but we need to know where they are headed so we can provide the teaching support to help them get there.

Prewriting
Finding Ideas for Writing Projects

One morning during writing workshop, we overheard Ashley saying to the other children at her table, "I just don't know what I'm going to work on next." While the problem she expressed is common enough, the language she chose to voice it is indicative of a very important understanding. Being concerned about what she'll *work on next* is different than being concerned because she doesn't know *what to write about*. The words show that Ashley thinks of writing as projectlike work. The ideas for writing are not just things to write about; they are ideas she'll use to make something.

We believe that the process of writing begins with finding ideas for the kind of writing you are planning on doing, for a writing *project*, so to speak, so this is where we'll expect students to begin. When we start writing workshop, students know what kind of writing they'll be doing—just as experienced writers know this—because we've told them that they'll make picture books at first. We believe that having this vision of what they'll make gets them searching for bigger ideas than just "something to write about." They need ideas for "something they'll make a book about." The difference is subtle, but it helps us get them leaning toward that understanding that experienced writers have, that the kinds of ideas we need have a lot to do with the kind of writing we are going to do; that is, memoirists need different kinds of ideas than fiction writers, who need different kinds of ideas than poets. . . .

Our youngest writers are expected, from day one, to make their own decisions about ideas for writing projects, and we find that they go about choosing their ideas in many of the same ways experienced writers do. They write about things they know about from everyday life—their families, pets, friends, play times, school. They write about their interests and passions—dinosaurs, animals, Barbies™, video games, fishing. They write about the same things over and over in lots of different books, and sometimes they make books for specific people and occasions in their lives. Our youngest writers also get a lot of ideas from each other—"I'm going to make a book about snakes, too, just like Cauley is making"—and this seems to be much more acceptable to them than it is to older students. Often, we find they work side by side on these books about the same exact topics.

And of course, it's important to remember that they don't need a new idea every day. Because they are making books, they have an investment in their ideas that is bigger than a single day's writing. Following through on the guidelines for finishing a piece of writing takes most of them several days, and many of them have pieces in their folders that they work on in starts and fits over a very long period of time before they are finished (and some pieces never get finished). While we don't want them endlessly taking paper and starting new books that they never finish, we think it's fine for there to be some books in their folders that they work on off and on over time.

So, what support do we have in place for helping children with this part of the process? Some of our whole-class teaching off and on during the year will be about how writers get ideas for writing. In Section 3 (pp. 155–231) you'll read about a unit of study devoted specifically to this part of the writing process, and, of course, all genre study has some teaching about how writers of a particular genre get their ideas.

Other than this study, though, the biggest support comes in the form of *talk*. We are always talking about what the children are writing about and where they got the ideas for the books they're making. If we're looking at something a child has written during the minilesson or share time, we talk about the idea behind it. As we confer with individual children, we talk about where they got their ideas for the writing. When we look at published writing by professional authors, we talk about where we think the writers may have gotten the ideas for their books. As things are happening in our lives, we are thinking about what we *could* write about those happenings. And of course, the children talk among themselves as they work on their writing, and they get lots of

FIGURE 4.2 Robert and Steven talk about Robert's latest book.

ideas from each other. We also see that this talk is often extended beyond writing workshop time as they plan together—out at recess and on
the bus and at lunch—what they might do with writing. That sort of
planful talk is only possible when they know they can count on having
writing workshop time every day.

We really just don't see many students struggle for very long to
find ideas for books, and we think this is related, again, to the projectlike nature of the work they do during writing workshop. When a student is struggling to get started with something, we might encourage
her to walk about the room and see what other children are working on
in their books. This often helps get ideas going for a writer. We might
encourage the child to look through her folder and see if there is a piece
there she could revisit. We might also have a conference with the child
and help her find an idea using the understandings we know professional writers use to choose their ideas. If we came to a place in the year
where lots of children were struggling with finding ideas for books, we
would likely readdress the issue with another unit of study on finding
ideas for writing.

Prewriting
Growing Ideas for Writing Projects

Most experienced writers actually live with ideas for writing projects for
some time before they begin drafts. While they are in this living-with-
an-idea part of the process, they grow their thinking about the idea by

collecting all sorts of related, random thoughts, and sometimes by writing reflectively and extensively about the idea. If the project idea demands it, writers may be doing research to get specific information they'll need to do the writing. They may be reading to get a sense of the kind of writing they are planning to do. And most writers talk a lot about an idea for a writing project before they actually begin a draft of it. Often, with a draft in mind, they begin to organize their thinking in some way so that it starts to take shape.

Many experienced writers use a writer's notebook as a tool to collect all this thinking they do while they are living with an idea. The notebook is especially handy for quickly jotting down all those thoughts that come to writers when they are away from their desks and computers. Notebooks often travel with writers everywhere for just this reason: to capture that thinking. The writer's notebook is kept because the writer plans to do published writing from the material gathered in the notebook. This sense of future published writing is what sets the writer's notebook apart from a diary or journal that is kept just for the sake of keeping it.

For our youngest writers, for several reasons, we don't introduce writers' notebooks as a tool for future published writing at the beginning of the year. First, most of the children don't yet write fast enough to quickly jot down their ideas or to use writing to think out an idea because the idea comes so much faster than the writing. If they did write as fast as they think, they probably wouldn't be able to reread it, and then it wouldn't be a very effective tool. They'll need to develop some fluency before the notebook makes sense as a tool in this way.

The children also need to have a clear sense of what the notebook would be used for—published writing—for it to make sense as a *tool* for that. It would be very difficult for them to hold some vision of future writing they would do from the notebook writing if they'd never done anything but write in a notebook. So we need them to have made lots of books before we introduce them to a tool to help them make books.

And finally, developmentally, our youngest writers live sort of in the moment, so we don't expect them to live with an idea for very long before they begin the actual writing. As a matter of fact, most of the time they go directly from having an idea for a writing project right to the first page. During the year, we'll expect our teaching to nudge their development in this area somewhat. We'll teach them to talk a lot about an idea before they begin to write it, for example, and we'll encourage them to think about ideas when they're at home for books they are working on in school—as Cauley was doing with his missnake idea. We'll also teach them to do research for nonfiction and collect things to write from in poetry and memoir. But the bottom line is, until they develop the fluency to write fast enough to capture their thinking with written words, we have to stay focused in this part of the process on just using talking and thinking to grow their ideas.

In Section 3, as you read about units of study, you'll see that later in the year when children have lots of bookmaking under their belts, we might introduce the writer's notebook as a very specific kind of tool—a place to write facts to use in nonfiction or to capture observations for poetry, for example. It's still not writing to think yet, but it's certainly writing to gather and a starting place for understanding the notebook as a tool for published writing.

Prewriting
Planning for a Draft

As we said earlier, when they first begin writing, most children go straight from having an idea, to announcing they have it ("I'm gonna make a book about NASCAR"), to beginning the first page. And once they start, they make a lot of it up as they go, moving seamlessly between talking the idea, drawing the idea, and writing the idea. For our youngest writers, the intellectual and fine motor demands of *any* writing are such that to make some distinction between prewriting and writing seems a little ridiculous. It's all writing to them and it's all challenging and when they're doing it, they're just doing it—they're not getting ready to do it.

During the year we will teach children a little more about this part of the process and we'll help them see that there are some things they can do to get ready to write. But the challenges of this teaching are to keep it real—to keep it grounded in what we know about this part of the process from experienced writers—and to keep it developmentally appropriate. And it is the combination of those two challenges that causes us not to push too far into this part of the process with our youngest writers.

We know that experienced writers use a variety of strategies to get a draft started—everything from just starting it and seeing where it goes to planning it out in great detail—and that very few writers use the same strategy for every piece of writing. Sometimes, the getting-started strategies have a lot to do with the kind of writing it is.

Our youngest writers are pretty good at just starting it and seeing where it goes. But when we think about the other extreme—planning a piece of writing out in great detail before starting the draft—it just doesn't make much sense for them. For one thing, their pieces of writing aren't that long. An exhaustive plan for writing is usually made when there will be a lot of volume to the writing and a lot of different parts the writer will have to manage. Another thing is that many of the books our youngest writers make are really just lists of ideas about a topic, separated into different pages. How would they outline that? What would be the difference between outlining it and just writing it? If they don't like the order of it once it's written, then a staple remover can solve that problem.

We know that in many classrooms, children fill out little story frames or graphic organizers before they write. We have just not found these to be very useful because we believe we give up more than we get in children's understanding of process when they use them. We get nice, orderly pieces of writing from story frames. But, as we said before, we know that experienced writers don't have some set way that they always start a draft—they have a variety of ways of doing this—and we just don't want to use a tool for writing that might communicate an over-simplified message about this to children. We would rather the children do what writers really do, and do it like six-year-olds in all their wonderfully approximated ways, than to give them some artificial tool to use until they become experienced. We also don't want to limit them just to writing pieces in the mold of a few select frames. This also oversimplifies the process because deciding how something will go is an important part of the evolution of writing.

Probably our biggest teaching into this part of the process is our close look at different ways to structure texts. As children learn that texts are structured in different ways and they begin to try out different ways of structuring their own texts, many of them begin to think ahead about how the whole book will go. Katie happened upon Jordan one morning when he was working on a book about his dog, Sunny, using a question-and-answer structure that is very common in the predictable books he was reading at the time. He was only one page into the book, but when Katie asked him what he was working on, he proceeded to tell her how the whole book was going to go up until the end, where you would find Sunny tied up to a tree.

The idea of having a structure for his writing had given this very beginning writer a sense of his text as a whole, and he used it to see into the future of his writing. This is so critical. We believe that the planning experienced writers do comes from them being able to see into the future of their writing, and we have come to believe that the best work we can do with our youngest writers (in terms of planning) is to give them visions of what's possible in texts. While we'll still do most of this planning with talk, as the year progresses, we'll talk more and more about what we're *going* to do in our books, and this talk will be the mainstay of our prewriting diet.

FIGURE 4.3 Jordan's question-and-answer book about his dog, Sunny. (1) Where is Sunny? Illustrated by Jordan and words by Jordan. (2) Where is Sunny? Is he in his doghouse? No. (3) . . . is he under the bed? No. (4) . . . is he running around? No.

FIGURE 4.3 *continued* (5) . . . is he playing? No. (6) . . . is he tied up to a tree? Yes.

Drafting and Revision

Drafting and revising, that slippery part of the process where we get our ideas down on the page and work with them until they're just the way we want them, is challenging for even the most experienced writers. But imagine meeting that challenge when you also have to think about the spelling (and the formation of individual letters) for almost every single word you put on the page—something that is so automatic for experienced writers that they think almost nothing about it when writing. If they are using word processors, they think about these mechanics even less. In many ways, beginning writing really feels more like beginning *spelling*, and we guess because of that, some believe we should just teach them to spell first and let their skill with composition come later. We don't believe that, of course; we believe the two can develop simultaneously, but even so, we can't ignore the developmental importance of getting the words down on the page in beginning writing. Understanding this important stage of development leads us in a number of instructional directions with our youngest writers.

Getting the Words Down on the Page

First of all, early in the school year, we'll need to help the children think a lot about how they'll get words down on the page. Now this is drafting work, not editing work yet, and our goals for it are simple. First, we want the children to be able to generate a spelling (it needn't be conventional) for any word they want and then be able to read that word back after they've written it. And second, we want them to be able to do this with as little disruption to their thinking about their ideas as possible. We want them to be able to do it quickly, in other words. It takes some experience with writing before they consistently meet both these goals. Some will come to us in first grade with that experience already, but many of them won't, so at first we just need to get them working in that direction with writing.

To this end, in her first unit of study, Lisa introduces her young writers to a few simple, universal tips for getting words down on the page. She tells them

- Think about what the word looks like. If you think you've seen it before, try to picture the letters in the word.

- Think about what the word sounds like. Say it aloud slowly and listen to the sounds in the word and think about the letters that could represent those sounds.

- Think about whether it is a long or short word. Do you need just a few letters to make this word, or a lot?

- Think about other words you know. Is this word anything like another word you know?

- Ask yourself, Is this word somewhere in the room where I could easily find it?

She encourages them to use these strategies to get the best spelling down that they can and then keep going with the idea. She also teaches them to reread what they've written often so they can keep the flow of the idea going and so they can remember what the words say. Again, doing this successfully and consistently is something that will take time for many of them. We know that in the beginning, many of them may write words one day that they aren't able to read (nor are we) the next day. If we're there when they encounter this problem, we help them reconstruct, as best we can, what it *likely* says and keep them going. In addition to this, when working one-on-one with children, we'll often jot a transcription in our notes of anything we think might be a problem for later rereading.

As children begin using strategies to help them get words down on the page, we must watch very closely to see that they are maintaining a productive level of attention to spelling. We don't want them to be so overly conscious about it that they're writing very little, and we don't want to see them not thinking about it all and just randomly putting letters on the page.

Our youngest writers know thousands and thousands of words and have made these words a part of their oral speech. Many of these words are not ones they would recognize in print yet in their reading, but we want them to be able to use these words in their writing. To help nudge them to do this, Lisa has developed a simple ritual for celebrating when children tackle words that are challenging to spell. A chart in the room reads "I'm not afraid of my words!" and when someone is caught being a fearless speller, the word the child tried is listed on this chart. During share time the class will look at the word and the writer will explain how he or she thought of the spelling. Then Lisa will show the children the conventional spelling and they'll either celebrate how close the writer came or marvel at how different the spelling is from what the writer thought it would be. It's a celebration either way, because the focus is on not being afraid to try a hard word you know, not on getting the spelling right.

So a lot of our earliest teaching about drafting is about getting the words we want down on the page. But as soon as we have almost everyone up and at least trying to do this, we are going to turn our attention to giving students a strong vision for what they might do with these words.

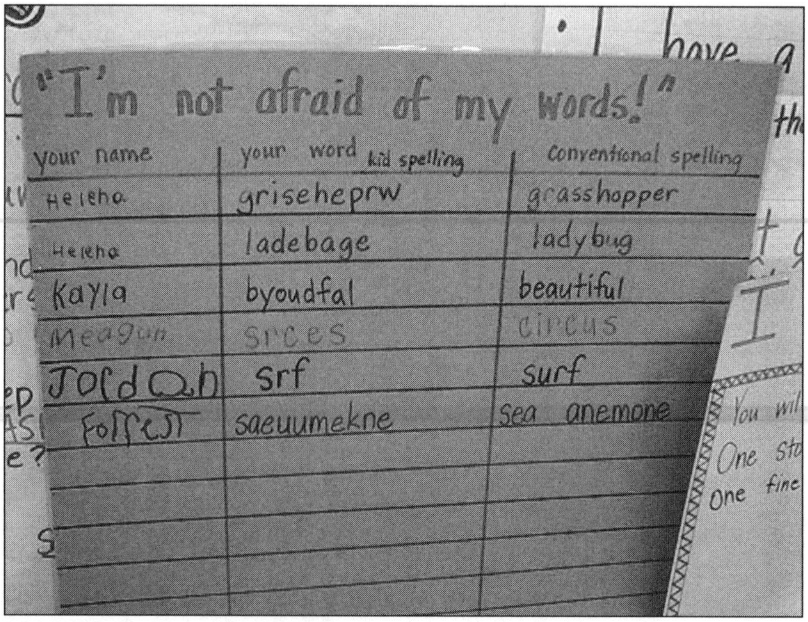

FIGURE 4.4 The "I'm not afraid of my words!" chart.

Re*vision* Begins with a Strong Vision

For most experienced writers, revision is a fairly intense process of reading and rereading and rereading a text. The writer is listening for where the writing sounds right and where it doesn't, where words and the ideas they represent ring true and less than true. "Is this really what I meant to say?" The writer is focusing on the meaning of every single sentence and making sure that one sentence leads as effortlessly as possible to the next. The writer is looking at the big chunks of ideas and making sure the journey from beginning to middle to end works in the way the writer intends. The writer who is revising is riding on a time machine of sorts as he makes the move from thinking of the text as something he is writing (present), to thinking of it as something that will be read (future). He is trying to understand the text as it exists in both these times. It's a very complex thought process.

Some experienced writers revise a lot as they are drafting; others prefer to get the whole draft down and then go back through and revise. Most writers do some combination of both, making the lines between drafting and revision rather indistinct. In the process of revision, there are really just five things a writer can actually do to a text: change (rewrite) something, add something, take something out, move something around, or chuck it all and start over. Deciding which of these to do and how and where to do them is the intense part of revision; the mechanics of actually making the revisions has been made *incredibly* easy with the technology of word processing.

As we said earlier, getting the words down on the page the first time is intense intellectual work for our youngest writers. It follows, then, that since they are not writing on word processors yet, the mechanics of making revision changes, particularly of rewriting something by hand, is a big, big task. Recognizing this, and the complexity of thought that leads to revision decisions, we simply do not push our youngest writers to do lots of revision work, particularly rewriting. Instead, we focus on text changes that are mechanically easy to make, and we teach hard toward a strong vision for the first—and often only—draft.

Once children are up and writing, we can introduce them to the idea of adding something by simply adding words underneath or above those already written, using a caret to insert words inside a sentence, using a sticky note, or taking the staples out and adding in whole new pages. We may also show them that moving pages around (so they are in a different order) or taking something out is as simple as taking staples out or casting a line through something. As we show students these revision possibilities, we will likely talk to them about the reasons writers have for making these kinds of changes. We might even slow a certain kind of revision thinking down—such as when to add to writing—and address it as a unit of study.

Again however, we recognize that knowing *when* to make changes like these requires a whole other layer of complex thinking that is difficult to maintain while you are thinking about so many mechanical issues as you generate text. Sometimes children will decide to make these kinds of revisions on their own, but more often than not they make them with some guidance when we are conferring with them. As they talk with us about what they're writing, we listen to see if any natural revision possibilities present themselves and if they do, we sometimes suggest the child try something. For example, for Jordan's book about Sunny that we saw earlier in this chapter (Figure 4.3), suppose Jordan showed us what he was working on and told us that it was very dusty under the bed where Sunny sometimes hides. We might suggest he add that detail so it would read, "Where is Sunny? Is he on the dusty floor under the bed?" We would explain how it would make a different impression on the reader if it were clear that Sunny might be in all that dust.

Young children's talk around their writing is always bigger than the actual words on the page. We embrace this developmental truth and let them talk and talk about the bigger ideas that are connected to their writing but aren't represented with words. Our goal is never to get the writing to capture all the details of their thinking. That would be too overwhelming. But we do know that contained within this talk, there are many opportunities to help them do a kind of simple, additive revision. The challenge is to recognize when to start nudging them to add and how much nudging is enough and how much is too much. We try to make this judgment based on the child's developing fluency, recognizing it might take as much as several years of experience before children can really be expected to make their written texts as big as their thinking around them.

Of course, many books get written and we aren't there in a conference as the children are writing them, and of course, we don't always suggest a child try some revision work in our conferences, so many books are written during the year with no revision work done on them at all. We are careful in the work we do decide to do with revision to help children develop healthy attitudes about this part of the process. We don't want them to think of it as something they need to do because they didn't try hard enough the first time. We want them to think of adding in, moving around, and taking out as another interesting part of the work of making books.

The other main way we work with revision is to help children have a strong *vision* for the writing they are doing when they set out to get it down on the page the first time. Most of the writing you see in this book was written with little or no *revision*, but with lots of vision. Take Josh's piece about mammoths in the very opening chapter, for example. Think again about how clear his sense of what kind of thing he's making is, and of all the specific visions he has for what's possible in this kind of writing. In a very real sense, we believe that all the mini-lessons we teach that show children possibilities for ways to craft their writing are in the service of helping them draft with ever-clearer visions of what's possible in texts. And the clearer a writer's vision is as she's drafting a text, the less revision she will need to do later.

Editing

We'll use the word *editing* to refer to a writer's work on the most mechanical aspects of writing, much as we would use the word *proofreading*. Most experienced writers edit their writing continuously as they are also drafting and revising. They aren't concerned about it as they're in the heat of drafting, but most of the time when they see little changes that need to be made—a missing or an extra word, an apostrophe left out, a pronoun that doesn't agree with its antecedent—they will quickly make these changes right away. There is usually a last round of checking to be sure everything is in order before something is sent away, but often many bugs have already been addressed. Sometimes there is another experienced writer who gives a piece one last editing check.

There are two important things to remember about how experienced writers engage in this part of the process. First, in the real world in which we write, technology takes care of a whole lot of this editing work for writers, checking both spelling and grammar and offering helpful, specific suggestions for changes that can be made with the touch of a button. This technology has revolutionized this part of the process even more than it has revision, because with revision the writer still has to do the intense thinking about what changes need to be made. Not so with editing. Whether this is a good thing or a bad thing for the state of the language is a matter of personal belief, but the fact is, experienced writers have to pay far less attention to editing than they did when everything was written by hand or on typewriters. The children we are teaching will grow to be experienced writers in *this* world, not the one many of us knew as students. And who knows what other writing technologies might become available to them in their lifetimes?

Understanding this about how experienced writers edit simply helps us keep this part of the process in what we think is proper perspective. Certainly we want children gaining more and more control over the conventions of written language, and we'll address this off and on often throughout almost every school day. After all, the more writers know about how the language works, the easier technology will be to use. As a matter of fact, we hope someday the children we teach will be smarter about language than their grammar checkers! But we also know that this is the one part of the writing process that will always be very easy to get help with. Learning to write well-structured, engaging pieces of writing that build big ideas, communicate specific information, or tell compelling stories is much harder writing work and something no computer can—as of yet—do for a writer. And so as teachers of our youngest writers, we try to always keep this understanding at the forefront of our work and spend the balance of writing workshop time on these more complex aspects of composition.

The other important thing to remember is that, without the help of technology, a writer can't edit for what he doesn't know about how the language works. In other words, we can only fix things we know need fixing. A writer completing a piece by hand who doesn't change a *me* to an *I* (when this is the convention) may not yet understand subject and object pronouns. She can do her most careful editing and reread the piece dozens of times and never catch this because she just doesn't know this convention. It follows, then, that the editing fixes we do make on our own are for things we had the understandings to have written conventionally the first time, but inadvertently, as we were in the heat of drafting and revising, didn't get down on the page that way.

Now, this understanding about experienced writers is incredibly important in our work with young children. The challenge in this teaching is always to discern whether or not children have the necessary understandings to make their writing more conventional when they reread it. When they first start writing—sometimes in kindergarten and often even long before that—they don't really own any firm understandings about language or spelling conventions with which they might edit, and so it would be very inappropriate to ask them to try. But with time and experience writing, and especially as they emerge and take off as readers, their understandings about these conventions will grow and we'll want to start nudging them to use these to do some beginning editing.

So as we work with our youngest writers, our guiding question as teachers will be, "What's in this piece of writing that, with a little specific attention, I think this writer would be able to make more conventional *on his own*?" Notice the language here: "make more conventional." When our youngest writers edit, it doesn't always mean they make changes that make the writing right in the same sense it would be if an experienced writer edited it. But that doesn't mean they aren't editing; they are still thinking like people who edit if they reread and alter something in the text because they want to make it more closely match what they understand about how writing goes down on the page. For example, the child who rereads and—probably based on visual memory—adds an *e* to his spelling of *fet* (*feet*) but adds it in the wrong place, *fete*, is in fact editing. We strongly encourage good intentions in editing when children first start trying it. We know their good intentions will lead to better and better results the more experience they get with both reading and writing.

We may actually start teaching the habit of mind of editing—rereading to see if everything is as it needs to be on the page—with some simple things that have more to do with the layout of the books the children are making than with real understandings about the conventions of language. For example, we may ask them to check things such as these:

- Are all my pages in the right order?
- Do I have a date stamp and my name on the book?
- Do I need anything else in my illustrations?
- Did I make a title page for my book?

Questions like these can initiate children into the understanding that a writer goes back over a piece of writing carefully before finishing it, an essential understanding for them to become good editors.

Beyond this, we know it's time to start nudging children to edit for actual language conventions when we see a few key understandings manifesting themselves consistently in their writing. These understandings give the children a starting place in their attempts to edit. These understandings are the ones we'll talk about and demonstrate again and again as we look at and use writing all day long in many different contexts. These understandings are the ones we'll often help children learn to control as we work with them side by side in conferences as they're writing. And when we really see them begin to write with these understandings comfortably guiding them, it's time to introduce editing. Some of them will come to us ready for this at the beginning of first grade, and others will take most of a school year to really own these understandings.

Editing for Spelling

First, we need to see that they are spelling with a variety of strategies—using visual memory of a few high-frequency words, sound-symbol knowledge, word length, knowledge of other words, and so on. Their writing needs to show a clear sense of "wordedness," with spaces separating the words. When these two understandings are in place and seem to feel comfortable for children, we can begin to ask them to look for two things when they reread a piece:

- Do I have all the words I need on this page? Am I reading words that aren't actually there? I can use my finger to move underneath each word I say to check this. I need to add in any words I realize I meant to write but didn't.

- As I'm reading what I've written, do I see any letters that seem to be missing or need to be changed in any of my words? If I do, I can add these on the end, squeeze them in the middle, or strike a line through some and write new letters above them.

We'll begin with these expectations, but over time as children become confident spellers, we'll want to be more specific. We'll introduce the children to the concept of high-frequency words and let them know we want them to use their visual memory, the resources in the room, and strategies like have-a-go (trying the word several times to see which spelling looks right) to get these spellings under control. We'll also explain that if there is a challenging word they are going to use again and again in a book, perhaps a word like *camouflage*, they might want to get help with spelling that word since they'll be using it often. It is important to note that we don't expect first graders to finish pieces of writing and then edit for all the spellings in the whole piece. Instead, we want to see that they have done a good job of editing for spelling using the beginning understandings they have. Beyond this, we realize that if they are writing with all the richness of the words they own in their oral vocabulary, many of these will be words they've rarely if ever seen in print. We believe the burden of having to fix the spellings of all these words is developmentally inappropriate.

Editing for Punctuation

Once it becomes clear that children understand there are marks in writing that aren't letters but do another kind of writing work—punctuation marks—we can begin to ask them to think about these marks as they reread. Our first charge to them will likely be a very simple one like this:

- As I'm rereading my piece, do I see that I've used enough punctuation in it to help people know how to read it? If not, I need to add marks where I think they will help.

We are not at this point aiming for consistent accuracy in the use of punctuation, but for thoughtfulness about its use and evidence of ever-deepening understandings about it.

Once we see that children understand the sentence as an essential unit in writing and they are punctuating sentences fairly consistently with end marks, they are ready to begin editing for capitalization. Of course, they also need to understand the difference between lower- and uppercase letters to do this editing work. Our charge to them for capitalization will be something like this:

> • As I'm rereading my piece, do I see that I begin my sentences with capital letters? If not, I need to strike a letter out and capitalize it. Are there any other words that are names for things that might need to be capitalized?

These really feel like the beginning editing essentials and they get at all the expectations for editing listed in our state's standard course of study for first grade. We'll look for ways to help children make these kinds of editing changes easily. We don't mind if their books are messy with editing changes—strikeouts and letters and words squeezed in between others. In fact, we like to be able to see the evidence of their editing. We also introduce sticky notes as a tool for editing, especially for spelling. That's what Tayler used to edit the spellings of two high-frequency words on a page from her book *I Went Everywhere* (see Figure 4.5).

Just as with revising, we'll work with children around editing a lot in our individual conferences with them. We'll use what we know about them as readers and writers to help us discern when and where to nudge them to reread and try to make their writing more conventional. And, again, our goal is not to have perfectly edited pieces of writing when children are finished. Our goal is to see in a piece that a child has deliberately used what he knows about the conventions of spelling and language to write this piece as well as he can.

Our hope is that by the end of the year, we'll have most of the children writing fluently and controlling these most basic editing skills fairly consistently. If we can get them to this developmental place where they are comfortable with these basic conventions of written language, then they'll be ready in the next years of school to begin thinking about the more sophisticated language understandings that writers use to edit—subject-verb agreement, pronoun usage, specifics

FIGURE 4.5 Tayler uses sticky notes to edit for spelling. (1) I went walking in the desert. It was very hot. (2) Spelling corrections made with sticky notes.

of punctuation—understandings that will develop over time as they read and write more and more each year in school.

Publishing

Many of the books the children finish are not published in any more formal way. They are simply finished and shared and that's the end of it. Remember that we have set the children up to put a lot of energy into the production of books right from the start, so to ask the children to reproduce them in the name of publishing in the end just doesn't make much sense. As a result, many of their end products will look very much like something six-year-olds have written. Some of these books will go to the audiences for whom they were written, some may go in different places about the room if they're a good example of some craft technique or smart work, and some will simply stay in the children's folders until we clean them out and they go home.

Some of the children's finished writing may go out in the hallway. We know that the culture of hallways in schools varies a lot. We are lucky that in the hallways at Jonathan Valley Elementary, it is OK for the work posted there to look like six- and eight- and ten-year-olds did it.

It is OK for it to look like the work of children who are *learning how to write.*

When the children's work is put in the hallway, it's a good idea to put a note underneath it directing readers' attention to what's really smart in the writing, something like, "Look . . . Tayler wrote her book and used a repeating line to tie vignettes together." If it's a variety of work from different children from a unit of study, there may be a note about the study, something like, "Our class has been studying text structures. Look at the variety of ways we've learned to structure our texts!" And then underneath each child's piece, we can name the structural device used. Posting children's writing in this way can do a lot of work to educate others who don't really understand the writing work we are doing in our classrooms because it directs their attention to the smartness in the work.

One option that does exist in Lisa's writing workshop is that of "fancy" publishing. All this really means is that a book gets typed out on the computer. Once Lisa is comfortable that a child has done all she can with a piece of writing, the child may opt for fancy publishing. This is usually done with an adult. The child takes the piece and the two sit side by side at the computer and make decisions about page layout, font, size, color, and so on as the text is entered into a word processing document. All the spellings the child didn't fix on her own during editing are fixed, and there is often a lot of talk about where the punctuation should go as the text is being entered. The talk around fancy publishing is actually a rich teaching opportunity as the child and the adult look closely at how the text will go down on the page. Children can certainly use the computers on their own to fancy publish, and if they do, the end product will look like six-year-olds using computers to write. Once the pages are printed out, the child reillustrates the book.

In most years, we have not found that there are more children wanting to fancy publish than Lisa and her assistant, Angie (and the occasional classroom volunteer or university intern), can handle. Most of them finish lots of books and show no desire to do this more formal type of publishing. If there were lots of them wanting lots of fancy publishing, we would simply make a rule limiting the number of pieces a child may choose to publish in this way.

Sometimes we encourage children to fancy publish a book because we want this publishing to support their reading and writing development. Jordan's nonfiction book *Guinea Pigs Need Room to Play* was a book we encouraged him to fancy publish. The book showed several sophisticated understandings Jordan had learned as we studied nonfiction and text structures, so it was an important benchmark in his learning for

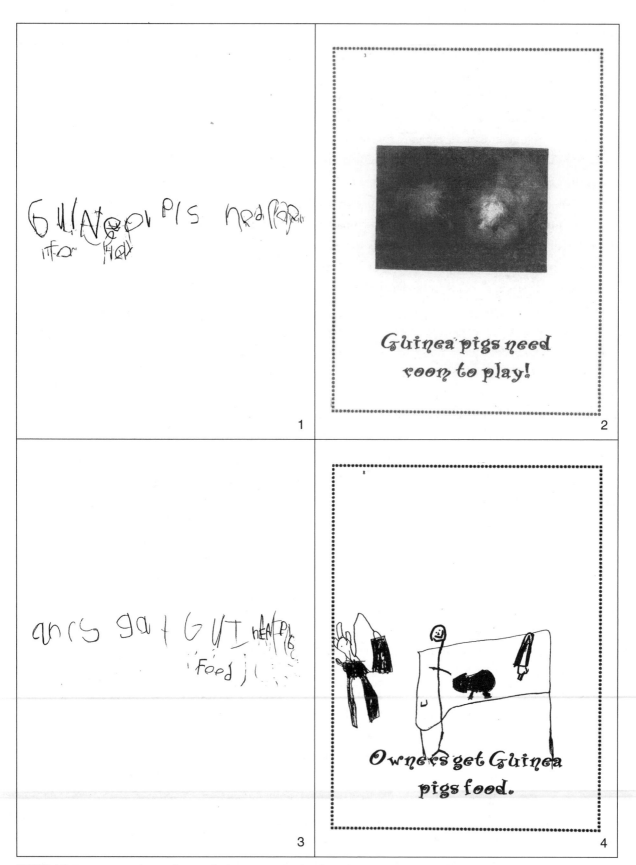

GUINEPVPIS nnaPaP
itfa' Ha

Guinea pigs need
room to play!

anrs ga t GUINEAPG
Food

Owners get Guinea
pigs food.

1	2
3	4

FIGURE 4.6 Two excerpted pages from Jordan's guinea pig book—first as he wrote them, then fancy published.

the year, but the book was difficult for him to reread. Publishing it on the computer gave him access to it as a reader and allowed him to join more easily in the abundant sharing of nonfiction we did around this study.

We should note that many of the most beginning writers finish books during the year that are difficult to reread. We aren't uptight about this and don't ask them to fancy publish all of these. We encourage a child to do this (if he hasn't decided to on his own) only if the piece is an important book for the child to come back to again and again for some reason, or if the piece is going to an outside audience who would be completely baffled by the child's approximations in the original writing.

Closing Thoughts on Process

The children in Lisa's writing workshop don't follow the steps of the writing process as if they were following the kind of incredibly specific directions you get from MapQuest when you are going on a trip. Instead, the process for them is a mostly joyful, meandering journey they take from having an idea all the way to completing a finished piece of writing. We walk along beside them or just behind them as they wander on this journey, helping them when they seem to need a little help finding their way, and always, always marveling at the fascinating writing destinations to which they lead us.

CHAPTER 5

Looking Closely at Minilessons

Whole-Class Teaching That Fills the Workshop with Possibilities

Looking through books for sale at a writing conference, Katie comes across G. Brian Karas' picture book *Atlantic* (2002). After reading only the opening page or two, she thinks to herself, "Oh my, I have to buy this for Lisa's class. They need to see this."

Two things in particular strike her about the book. One is the first-person narration. Lisa and her students have become very interested in first-person narration during the year, but they have looked mostly at books with animals speaking as narrators. In *Atlantic*, the ocean is given a voice and allowed to speak its own story. Katie knows that it will deepen the students' understanding of first-person narration to see something inanimate speaking in the same way. There also are some fabulous verbs on that first page or two and Katie knows that this is something of interest to Lisa's students as well.

> I *stretch* from the icy poles
> North and South
> I *rub* shoulders with North America
> and *bump* into Africa

She buys the book, believing Lisa's students really *need* to see it.

Our Teaching Stance

We find that we move through the world this way, always on the lookout for books and materials we can bring to our minilessons that will help our students see new possibilities for writing or deepen the understandings they already have of what's possible. As teachers of writing, we believe that one of our primary jobs is to help children build a repertoire of possibilities, a repertoire of things they know they can try when they write. We want them to go out to write each day in a room filled with the energy of ideas, an energy that says *Look at this. Look at what this writer is doing. This is so cool—somebody in here could try this, you know.*

In this chapter we want to think about how our minilessons—the ten- to fifteen-minute lessons that start each day's writing workshop—help create that "somebody could try this" energy around children's writing. As we've stated before, these minilessons are organized into specific units of study, and in the next chapter we'll think through that organization. But first, we want to look at what matters most in these lessons and name the predictable ways we go about the teaching.

Setting the Stage: Listening Like People Who Make Books Too

One morning during a study of making illustrations and text work together in powerful ways, Lisa's university intern, Emily, is leading the students in looking at all the decisions Joanne Ryder (author) and Norman Gorbaty (illustrator) made in their picture book *Earthdance* (1996). Right in the middle of the lesson as students notice words wrapped around a picture of a hillside, Kayla thinks aloud, "Hey, I could put words like that in the wheel in my hamster book." Emily honors this comment and asks Kayla to explain what she's thinking, slowing the lesson down so students can watch Kayla in the act of envisioning possibilities for her own writing.

This kind of connection, from seeing something in a book to imagining it as a specific possibility for someone in the room, happens all the time and is one of the most important big ideas that informs all teaching across the year. If we ask students in Lisa's room to tell as about what happens in their minilessons each day, most of them will give some version of the same answer: "Well, we talk about ideas and stuff we can do when we write." They think of the lessons as having this purpose each day—to give them ideas about what they can try in their writing. Not topic ideas for what to write about—they already have those, as Kayla did with her hamster book—but ideas for *how* to write things.

The seeds for children thinking of minilessons in this way—as naturally and effortlessly as Kayla did on this morning—are planted early in the year. Remember that one of the first things we help young writers realize is that they make books, too. We staple the paper together so it looks like a book because right from the start we want them to think of themselves as people who make books. We are careful to name students' writing moves as being like the moves of professional writers they know so they see themselves in this way. When Lisa tells Marissa her illustrations remind her of Byron Barton's illustrations because they are outlined in black, she's helping this six-year-old see herself as being like this other person who does what she is doing.

We keep coming back to this point about identity again and again because we just can't get away from how significant it is to the learning we see. When students bring their identities as people who make books with them to the carpets of our minilessons, they look at what Joanne Ryder and Norman Gorbalty are doing altogether differently. They *listen*

FIGURE 5.1 Kayla puts words inside her illustration of the hamster wheel.

so differently to the teaching because of these identities they have. Everything they see in books becomes a possibility, a thing someone might try because, hey, after all, *We do this stuff too. We make books too.*

So before students can even begin to think in the ways Kayla was thinking, they have to see themselves in this way. They also need to have seen demonstrations of this kind of thinking. Early in the year we have to demonstrate a lot of the kind of thinking—which we call *envisioning*—that Kayla was doing. We do it for them. We show them how to go from something we see a writer doing into envisioning it as a possibility for their own writing. For example, if the students notice that Frank Asch's book *The Earth and I* (1994) begins and ends with the same line, "The Earth and I are friends," we say, "You know, someone in here could do that in a book. Like, let's see, Cele, you might do it in your book about buildings. You know how you say on the first page, 'There are all kinds of buildings,' and then you show all different kinds on the next pages? Maybe you could end it with that same line, 'There are all kinds of buildings,' just like Frank Asch did." We "write" something aloud when we envision so the children can hear what it would sound like if someone tried this in his or her writing.

Throughout the year, every time we look at books or listen to what professional authors have to say about writing, we are careful to help the children envision new ideas for their work from what we see and hear. When we do this thinking aloud with children we are really planting two different possibilities. One is for something a writer might try, a craft move (beginning and ending a text with a repeated line in the example above), but the other more important possibility is simply that a writer can think in this way. A writer can see something in a book and then think about doing it in her own work. Of course, again, a writer has to have some work going on of her own—some bookmaking—for this to make any sense. So early in the year we get them making books and we demonstrate this line of thinking and envisioning for them over and over and, in doing so, we set the stage for all our teaching across the year.

Minilessons as Predictable Teaching

As we think about planning for minilessons, we realize there are some predictable kinds of things we teach (curriculum) and some predictable ways we go about the teaching (methodology) in all the various units of study across the year. In fact, in terms of the nature of curriculum and methodology, what we do with our youngest writers is not really different from what we'd do if they were fifth graders or eighth graders or college students. What's different is the envisioning part. Every minilesson should end with students envisioning a new possibility for their work, and the key to successful minilessons is helping the group of students sitting in front of us to envision the difference this lesson might make in *their* work. As teachers, we have to think very specifically about this: "What would this look like if Meagan tried this? What difference would it make if Colten understood this?" So, with this in mind, let's take a look now at the kinds of things we teach and the predictable ways we go about teaching them to our youngest writers.

Before we walk through what's predictable in the curriculum and methodology of our minilessons, we should reiterate one point here and make sure it's clear. The purpose of minilessons is not to establish some writing task for the children to do during writing workshop each day. Remember that we begin the year by teaching them simply to go out and make books. They don't need us to give them any more work than that each day: go out and work on your books. The purpose of our minilessons, instead, is to fill the room with ideas for how they might do that bookmaking better and better.

Kinds of Things We Teach

We'll group the predictable kinds of things we teach into five broad categories: techniques, strategies, understandings, conventions, and questions. Understanding the nature of content in this way helps us envision more easily what difference it should make in our students' work as writers and why we are teaching it in the first place.

We define *techniques* as all the things writers know how to do with both text and illustrations (word choice, sentence structure, punctuation, paragraphs, text structures, genre specifics, etc.) to make the writing good. Techniques are basically the craft of writing. When Katie bought *Atlantic* for Lisa's students, she bought it because of the techniques she saw on the first few pages—the strong verbs and first-person narrator. When the students talk about Donald Crews' use of ellipses in *Sail Away* (1995) or how Cynthia Rylant repeats the word *borrowed* four times in the opening sentence of her book *Scarecrow* (1998), they are talking about techniques of writing. Lots and lots of minilessons during the year will present possibilities for crafting techniques students might use in their books to help them write well.

Strategies offer students possibilities for how to go about *doing* something while they're in the process of writing. For example, when we teach the children to reread everything in a book they're working on before they start writing more in it each new day, we're teaching them a useful strategy. When we teach them to read their texts aloud and listen for where the punctuation should go, make notes of facts they want to use in a piece of nonfiction, or talk an idea through with a friend before writing about it, we are teaching them strategies—ways to make the writing process they are using more efficient.

We define *understandings* as things to know about how writing happens (not things to do, like strategies, just important things to know), and they represent the big ideas underneath much of what we teach. For example, if we teach children that writers get ideas for writing out in the world or think about projects they are working on when it's not writing time, we are teaching them important understandings about writing. We'll reinforce many of the big understandings—writers read differently than other people, writing exists in many different forms and genres, writers think about their audience—again and again in different lessons across the year.

Conventions are ways to expect things to go in writing, ways that written language generally goes down on the page. The formation of contractions, capitalization, punctuation, and spelling are all conventions. While we'll teach a lot of our conventions on an individual basis in conferences or in the natural course of using language throughout the day, sometimes conventions are the subject of minilessons.

Finally, *questions* are lines of thinking that are useful for writers to follow. "How do I know when I need a peer conference?" and "How do I know if my book is finished?" and "What should I work on next in my writing?" and "Is there anything I could do to this writing to make it really good?" are examples of questions we might teach children to ask themselves again and again as they go about their writing.

Often, a minilesson will have more than one kind of content embedded in it. Take the lesson we mentioned earlier in the chapter when Cele's writing was used as an example for a writer trying the technique of repeating a line at the beginning and end of a text. The main content of the lesson is a technique possibility, but embedded in it are several important understandings: writers learn from what other writers are doing; this learning is not tied to topics, but to craft (Asch was writing about the earth and Cele about buildings); and writers often think through possibilities for what they're working on at any given time. As a matter of fact, most minilessons have layers of understandings about writing wrapped around the core content of the lessons themselves.

Ways We Go About the Teaching

While there are certainly some days that are exceptional, on most days what happens during the minilesson is fairly predictable. We have certain methods we use over and over again to get at the content and present students with possibilities that they can envision happening in their work. Let's think those through now, and then in the next chapter, as we think about organizing lessons into specific units of study, we'll be able to picture the teaching in these studies more easily.

Study Published Writing   Certainly more than anything else, we use published writing to show children possibilities during our minilessons. This published writing is usually the work of professional writers, but it may also be the work of children in the room or from years past. Either way, we look to this writing with one question in mind: *What can I learn from this that I might try in* my *writing?*

There seem to be three main ways we look at published writing. One is to just show students something. We have something we want them to see in a text, and we go right to it and show them. For example, in a study of how writers use punctuation in powerful ways, we might show students a sentence like this from Cynthia Rylant's *Christmas in the Country* (2002): "Every Christmas Santa gave me just what I wanted: a new doll." We'd explain to them how that wonderful mark, the colon, works, help them envision using one in their writing (we can either do this envisioning aloud or actually write an example), and then ask them to be on the lookout for colons as they read on their own and to try using one in their writing if it makes sense to do so.

A walk-through is another way we use published writing in minilessons. A walk-through is when we pull everyone in close and go through a book page by page, asking about each one, "What do you notice about how this is written?" When the question is fairly wide open like this, we may find ourselves talking about everything from who is narrating a text to how an illustration is rendered to why a sentence has

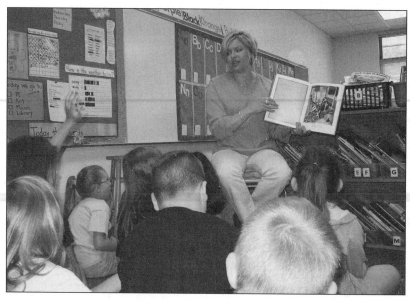

FIGURE 5.2 Lisa and the children study the craft of a picture book.

so many *and*s in it. With each new thing we see, we envision by talking about what it would sound like if someone in the room tried this in his or her writing. Often we focus our question more on a particular thing we are studying, "What do you notice about the punctuation in this book?" or "What do you notice that makes this nonfiction?" or "Which words really stand out to you as strong words?" If a particular book is really rich and full of things to look at, we may spend more than one day's minilesson walking through it and talking about all the possibilities we see in it for our own writing.

Almost always we use big charts to record the main things we're talking about as we walk through a book. Now, about these charts. In many ways they are more for us to use when we're teaching than they are for the children to use when they're writing. We don't see many of the children coming up to look at a chart and find an idea to try in their writing, though we know they've accessed these ideas somehow because we see so many of the ideas show up in their writing. We assume they just remember them. We're the ones who have trouble remembering, so our charts create a record of what we've talked about in these minilessons where we didn't know, going in, what our content would be because it would be generated by what the students noticed. We refer to these charts often in our minilessons and our conferences to help us make connections between the content and the students' writing and between the content of previous minilessons and current ones. And we expect, always, that the walls of the room will become heavy with charts and we'll have to take some down and replace them with others.

Small-group inquiry is the third way we use published writing in minilessons and when we do this, we have children look at books in small groups or pairs. Often, all the groups are looking at different books but with a single question guiding them. "What kinds of things does Donald Crews do in his illustrations?" or "What do you notice about poetry that is different from other kinds of writing?" or "Where do you see your writer making an interesting punctuation decision?" We usually give the children three or four sticky notes to mark the pages they most want to talk about when we come back together to share. Often, they'll write on the sticky notes what it is they've noticed.

Just as with walk-throughs, this kind of work usually stretches over more than one day's minilesson, we take time to envision the things they've noticed as possibilities for their own writing, and we often make charts to record what we've found. When we launch into work like this as part of the minilesson, what's interesting is that we don't know exactly what will come of it or what will be listed on our chart when we're finished. But we trust good writers to show us lots of possibilities, and

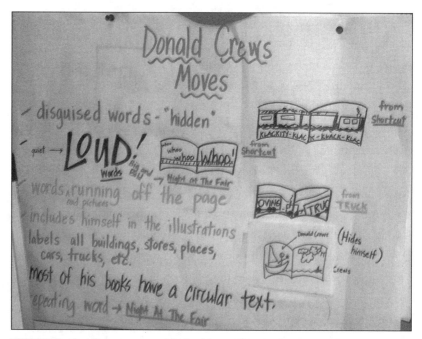

FIGURE 5.3 Chart from an ongoing study of Donald Crew's books.

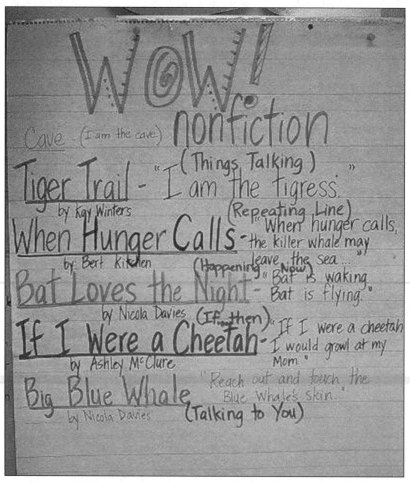

FIGURE 5.4 Chart from an ongoing study of literary nonfiction.

FIGURE 5.5 Children engaged in small-group inquiry.

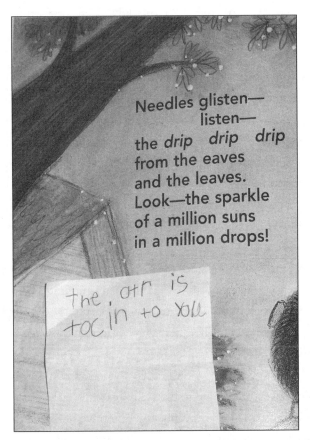

FIGURE 5.6 A sticky note of something the children noticed during inquiry. The note reads, "The author is talking to you."

we trust the children to notice them, so we don't worry much about the unknown.

Often, the published writing we use in minilessons is writing we have read before during read-aloud time or for some other content area purpose, but not always. Sometimes we read it as part of the minilesson, though this always takes up more time. Sometimes we actually revisit a book several times during the year for different purposes. We might look at the structure of it at one time, read it as an example of nonfiction another time, and look at the illustrations or punctuation during another study.

While most of what we get from published writing are possibilities for techniques for writing, sometimes we use published writing for other reasons as well. For example, in a study of where writers get ideas, we might walk through a stack of several books by a single author and see what understandings we can get from looking closely at this author's topic choices. Or we might show students a poem about a tornado, a nonfiction book about tornadoes, a story about a tornado, and an article in *Time for Kids* about tornadoes to help them understand that they might do several different pieces of writing from a single idea. And of course, for almost every book we encounter at any time of the day, we take a few moments to wonder, "How did this writer get this idea and what did she or he have to do to get this written?" This often leads us to important understandings about our own work as writers.

One thing seems important to mention here before moving on. We have found that it is not necessary for all or even most of the students in the class to be able to read the texts we're studying independently. Remember that both their oral (speaking and listening) vocabulary and their writing vocabulary will outpace their independent reading vocabulary. In other words, if we read them to them, they can understand books and consider the craft in books that they wouldn't be able to read yet on their own.

Study What Published Writers Say About Process   Another predictable way we teach in minilessons is to take strategies and understandings from what published writers say about the process of writing. We find what they have to say in some fairly predictable places: authors' notes, book flaps, forewords, afterwords, dedications, published videos, interviews, and websites. Anywhere a writer is likely to say something about how a certain piece of writing came to be, we're reading very closely to see what we might share with our students. When we do share, the lessons are fairly direct as we simply quote from an author and then, from the quote, help students envision possibilities for their work.

For example, in a genre study of poetry, we might read to the children from the afterword in Francisco X. Alarcón's collection *Laughing Tomatoes and Other Spring Poems* (1997), "I started writing poems by jotting down the songs my grandma used to sing to us. I would write at the kitchen table, surrounded by my pets, smelling my grandma's delicious cooking" (31). And after we read this, we would help them envision this happening in their own work as writers, writing poems at home themselves, listening to the language people are using there, responding to the sights and sounds all around them, just as Alarcón did.

In a study of where writers get ideas, we might read to them from the back book flap of Bob Graham's *"Let's Get a Pup!" Said Kate* (2001), "Our family once went to a dogs' home, looking for a small pup, and we came away with not one dog but two." Then we would help them envision that ideas for their stories could come from experiences they've had—visits to the hairdresser, first days of school, taking Sunday afternoon rides. Or in our beginning-of-the-year study of kinds of things to make in writing and how to make them in this room, we might share this quote from Jane Yolen's interview on Scholastic's website: "I never get writer's block because I write on a number of things at the same time. So that if one thing is not going well, I turn to another" (n.d.). We would then help them envision that sometimes, if they are having trouble working on a piece of writing, they might put it away for a while and work on something else.

We want the voices of writers the children know and love to be heard loud and clear in our minilessons across the year in our many different studies. When we honor these voices in our teaching, we see that as our students read new books, they think about the people who wrote them as familiar people, people a lot like them, and they wonder all about how these people did the writing they see. This connection to people who make books is a key to so much of their learning about writing.

Survey the Room Sometimes, to generate content for our minilessons, we survey the room and ask some or all of the students to answer some question about writing. We usually do this as we are sitting together in the meeting area for the lesson. When we survey the room, we do it because we are going to use their answers to help us form the content of our lesson, not because we are just trying to get them involved. For example, during a study of where writers get their ideas, we might ask each child to name the topic of the piece of writing he or she is working on at that particular time (or the last piece the child finished if he or she is in between). We would make a chart of these topics and then study the chart with the children to make meaning from what we see there. "What do you notice about the kinds of things we are writing about?" we would ask them. We would be searching for new understandings about where writers like us are getting ideas.

Most of our surveys of the room will help us get at understandings and strategies for the process of writing because we ask students to share with us what they do when they write. For example, we might use a survey of the room to find out what children are doing to generate challenging spellings, what kinds of things they think about when they reread something that is almost finished, how they decide where the punctuation should go in a book, or what kinds of help they ask other students for when they are writing. Occasionally, we will survey the room to find out what students already know about something we're going to study. We might ask them near the beginning of a poetry genre study what they think makes poetry different from other kinds of writing, for example, or ask them to say why they like the writing of their favorite authors at the beginning of a study of finding mentor authors.

Regardless of the question we choose to frame the survey of the room, the goal is always to learn something about writing—either the process of doing it or the writing itself—from what the children say. We turn their input into the content of the lesson, and because of this, just as when we plan a walk-through or an inquiry from published writing that we like, we don't know exactly what possibilities we'll end up with, but we trust that we'll end up with something.

Fishbowl   Sometimes we want students to watch an interaction around writing, often some kind of peer conference, and so we use a fishbowl technique to give them a vision of how the interaction should go. During the minilesson, the children actually watch something happen, as if they were peering into a fishbowl. They might watch two or three people helping another writer in a conference, for example. The people might be their classmates, their teachers, or older students who are experienced with conferencing. When the conference is over, we process it with them and focus on the important parts we want them to notice. We might point these out, or we might ask them what they noticed about the conference and then work from what they say. Either way, we need to end the same way we end every minilesson: by helping the children envision having a conference a lot like this in their own work as writers.

While we use the fishbowl most often to study conferences, we can actually use it to help students learn about any part of the writing process that can be outwardly observed. We might have the children observe a classmate who is particularly good at reading her writing aloud, for example, or listen to another who has developed a strategy for talking a book through before writing it. As we watch the students at work on their writing each day, we are always on the lookout for ways of working that we'd like others to see and that we might make part of future minilessons.

Teach from Our Own Writing   Sometimes in minilessons we use our own writing as the basis for the lesson. We think it is important that students see that we write too because it helps them to see us as being like them in that way. We might use our writing to show them how we tried a technique we are studying, or we might share strategies, understandings, and questions we use to help us with the process of writing. For example, in a study of how writers do research and grow ideas for writing, Lisa might read the children an excerpt from her writing about her dog Oscar and explain how she sat with paper in hand and watched him very closely, capturing all the specifics of his movement. The content of the lesson would be a strategy—you can take paper somewhere and observe something closely before you write about it— and she would help them envision doing this as they watched the streams behind their houses, their little sisters asleep, their fathers at work in the kitchen, and so on.

Every once in a while we will actually write in front of them in a minilesson, but we find the occasions for this are few in writing workshop. As we mentioned in Chapter 3, we write in front of them or interactively with them often during other parts of the day, thinking aloud with them about conventions and the composition of ideas as we write. But most of the time in minilessons during writing workshop, we are sharing the *thinking* about the writing more than the *act* of writing itself, so we share things that are already written. Even if we want to show them something like, say, how we decided between three different endings for a story or why we chose one particular word over another, we would likely have already written the story and then we'd simply talk them through how we made the decision about the ending or the word and help them envision thinking in these same ways about their writing.

Talk Out of Conferences   Finally, sometimes we just talk about something we have seen happening with writing as we have been conferring each day and observing the children at work. We might highlight something smart we see happening. For example, in a study of literary nonfiction, if we learn that Tayler went back and checked one of her facts about tigers because she was uncertain about it, we might have her tell the other students about this and explain how she knew to do this. Or, we might

FIGURE 5.7 Lisa and Robert teach the other children from Robert's conference.

address something that is not going well in the room. For example, in the same study of literary nonfiction, if we realize many children are copying directly from the books they're using for research and putting this info into the books they're making, we talk about this and then show them strategies to help them use these secondary sources in better ways.

To summarize, then, the following chart places these two ideas side by side:

KINDS OF THINGS WE TEACH	PREDICTABLE WAYS WE GO ABOUT THE TEACHING
• techniques	• study published writing: just show it, do a walk-through, small-group inquiry
• strategies	• study what published writers say about the process
• understandings	• survey the room
• conventions	• conduct a fishbowl activity
• questions	• teach from our own writing
	• talk out of conferences

Minilessons Teach Children How to Talk Like Writers

In early January, a little over a week after we've returned from the holiday break, the students are gathered for writing workshop and Lisa is talking to them about how she sees them doing so many things on purpose in their writing. Listen to the way she uses language as she talks to them about this:

> I see so many of you being so intentional about your decisions. You think about how you want every little thing to be in your books. I'm loving that you can tell someone the name of what you are doing—you can explain it.

And then she goes on to highlight some of the specific decisions children are making.

> Levi is making an illustration enclosed in a circle for the back cover of his books, just like Frank Asch does. Jordan is writing a book about Sunny (his dog) in a question-answer structure. Ashley is using photographs her grandmother sent her to help her write a book about her dogs, Cosmo and Babbette. Jared and Colten are coauthoring and illustrating, and so are Helena and Sierra. We need to keep at this—keep being intentional as we write. Let's all be sure to think about how we are going to write things and why we are writing them that way.

The language we use in our minilessons to talk about writing will become the language the students speak when they talk about writing. As a matter of fact, we are always struck by the fact that we can tell so much about writing instruction in a classroom without ever seeing any actual instruction. All we need to do is listen to what the children say about their writing. What words do they use to talk about what they are doing as they write?

We know that the way young children learn new words is to hear them used over and over in contexts that make sense to them. We also know that new words for new ideas help children think new thoughts. Many of the children in Lisa's room had never had anyone talk to them about being intentional in writing, or in anything else for that matter. But they were beginning to hear that word a lot during writing workshop and the word itself, *intentional*, helped them think in new ways about what they were doing. Lisa asked them often in conferences, "What are your intentions for this book?" And if she saw they still needed help with that concept, she asked it this way: "What are your intentions for this book? What are you thinking you are going to do with it?"—naturally layering in an explanation for the word just as she did several times in the previous excerpts from the minilesson.

We don't shy away from the words we need to talk about writing. We know that when they come to us, our youngest writers are likely to be unfamiliar with words and phrases like *genre* and *revision* and *text structure* and *verb* and *repetition* and *ellipses* and many others. But we also know that if we want our students to be writers, they need to speak the language that people who write speak. So we immerse them in that language, saturating our minilessons with all the words writers need to talk about how it all happens and how it all works.

We are careful to use the words most writers in the world use for the important concepts of writing. We don't call exclamation marks "happy marks" or periods "stop signs," for example. Some would say that terms like these are more kid-friendly, but we believe that if we embed kid-friendly explanations of what they mean as we use them (as Lisa did with *intention*), then we need not shy away from the words themselves.

We also feel strongly that as we study the techniques of craft with children, we should use the language of grammar whenever it makes sense to use it to help us describe what we see. If, for example, the children are noticing and talking about how Cynthia Rylant repeats the word *borrowed* four times in the opening sentence of her book *Scarecrow* (as we mentioned earlier in the chapter), we need to say, "Yes, look at that, she uses that same *adjective* four times in a row to describe his different parts—*borrowed, borrowed, borrowed, borrowed*—the same exact *adjective*." If we just embed words like this naturally into our talk around texts (and there are so many opportunities to do this), over time students will come to understand what these words mean. After all, why would we wait until third or fourth grade to call them adjectives if that's what we're talking about now, in first grade?

Now, after all that advice to make sure we use the real words for things, we should say that sometimes we find ourselves searching for words to help us explain something about writing when we don't know a word for what we're explaining. For example, one of the most common text structures we see in books is one in which a text moves back and forth in a predictable way between two kinds of information. We have a tub full of books structured just like this—*Tough Boris*, by Mem Fox, *Our Granny*, by Margaret Wild, *Daisy Thinks She's a Baby*, by Lisa Kopper, and lots more—but as far as we know, there isn't really a common name for this structure. So, to describe a text like this we have used the expression *seesaw text*. The children know exactly what it means and pick it out easily when they see a book that's written this way. They

FIGURE 5.8 In this excerpt from her book, *My Dogs and I Are Friends,* Ashley uses a seesaw structure to write about her two dogs.

6

Babbete is one year old.

8

Cosmo is brown, black and white.

Sometimes...

5

Cosmo is four years old.

7

Babbete is a black Lab.

FIGURE 5.8 *continued*

often structure their writing this way. In a conference with Ashley once, Katie asked her what the difference was between the book she was writing about her two dogs—Babbette and Cosmo—and the one she'd written about them a few months before. Ashley replied, "Well, this one seesaws and that one don't." And sure enough, it did (see Figure 5.8).

And of course, every year, with every group of children, we are likely to develop some particular language to talk about the things we're studying in writing along the way. We always love the insider's feel of language like this and we see it as very much a part of what makes each class its own community. The year Emily was teaching with Lisa, for example, "wrapping words around a picture like a sweater" became the classes' way of describing text in a picture book that is cropped tightly to an illustration. Emily was quite an accomplished knitter of scarves and sweaters, and all the children knew this, so when she used that expression to help give words to what they were noticing in a book, that particular way of saying it stuck with the class.

Our words matter, maybe more than we'll ever know. And in minilessons, where we do so much of the talking, we try our best to choose words both carefully and purposefully, knowing how much our talk supports the work of the young writers in the room.

Organizing for Thoughtful Instruction with Units of Study

It is early spring and Lisa is launching a new genre study of poetry in the writing workshop. The class is coming off some fairly heady work in its recent studies of illustrations and nonfiction, work that has helped Forrest—a natural lover of facts and information—find his wings as a writer. So Lisa is surprised during the early days of the poetry study when she has a conference with Forrest and he tells her, "I'm not very good at this poetry stuff. I think I'm gonna stick with nonfiction." When she asks him the logical question—how could he possibly (at the ripe old age of six) know he isn't good at poetry—he responds, "I don't know. I'm just not good at it."

Over the course of the next few weeks, Forrest will live out his days with his classmates in a writing workshop that is totally immersed in the study of poetry. He will be expected, as Lisa gently reminds him that morning, to write poetry, and a big part of our teaching job will be to help him see that he can, in fact, be good at it. With the help of poets like Kathleen O'Connell George and Nikki Grimes, Eloise Greenfield and Charles R. Smith, Forrest will soon see that poetry is just another form of writing he can use to write from his interests. The study takes hold of him, and before long he is sharing an NBA poem from his collection of sports poems as the children work at learning to read their writing so it sounds like poetry.

But Forrest's story doesn't end there. The next year he has moved on to second grade and has taken his new interest in the form of poetry with him. In his early writing work he chooses poetry as a way to write about his current topic of deep interest, birds. The decision to write poetry is one Forrest makes all on his own; his class isn't engaged in any new study of the genre.

The story of Forrest becoming a poet is the perfect story to show us why units of study matter so much in the writing workshop. In a span of months in his young life as a writer, Forrest went from being someone who thought poetry wasn't even an option to being a confident and skillful user of this wonderful form of writing. The weeks he spent immersed in the study of poetry left him able to envision many new possibilities as a writer.

In many ways, this is the driving force behind all units of study in the writing workshop. We want children to leave our studies able to

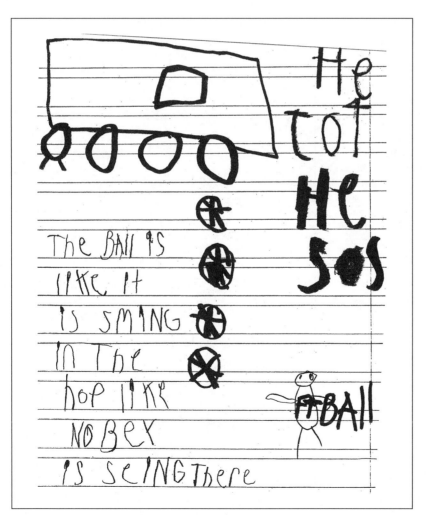

FIGURE 6.1 Forrest's NBA poem. The ball is / like it / is slamming / in the / hoop like / nobody / is standing there. / He jumped. / He shoots.

A Baild Ealg
orting
through
the
Siy
sorging, giding
swith And sjita
bassfsif
As can can Be
soting, dating
sole tade

A bald eagle
darting
through
the
sky
searching, gliding
swift and silent
as swift
as it can be
shooting, darting
slow landing

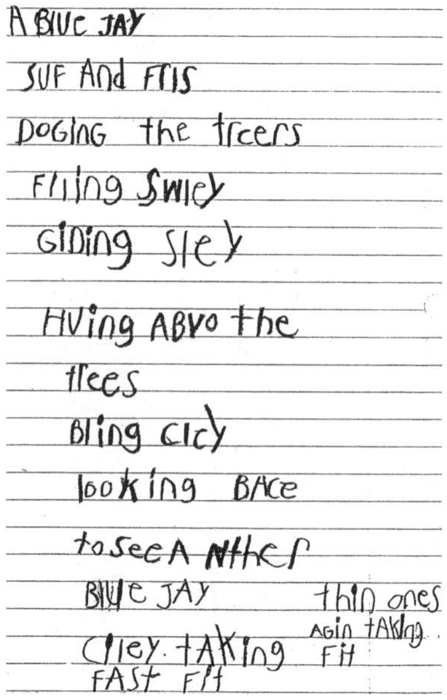

A Blue Jay
suf and ftis
doging the treers
fliing swiey
giding sley
hving abvo the
trees
bliing cicy
looking bace
to see a nther
blue jay
ciey. taking
fast fit
thin ones
agin taking fit

A blue jay
surfs and flies
dodging the trees
flying swiftly
gliding slowly
hovering about the
trees
Blinking clearly
looking back
to see another
Blue jay
clearly taking
fast flight
then once
again taking
flight

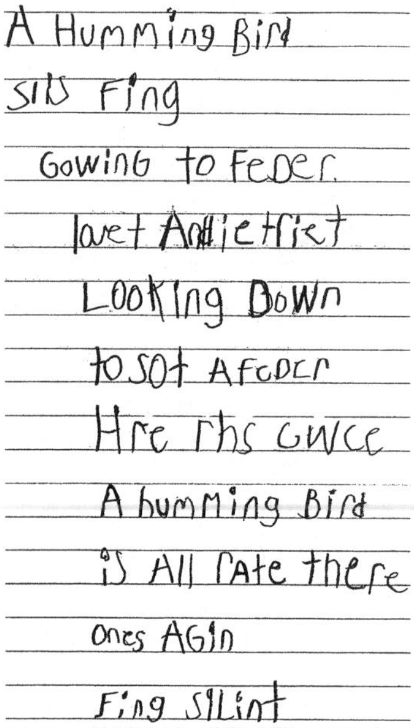

A Humming Bird
sis fing
gowing to feder
lavet andiethiet
Looking Down
to sot afeder
Hre rhs cwce
A humming bird
is All rate there
ones agin
fing silint

A hummingbird
is flying
Going to feeder
left and right
looking down
to spot a feeder
hurry rush quick
A hummingbird
is all right there
once again
flying silent

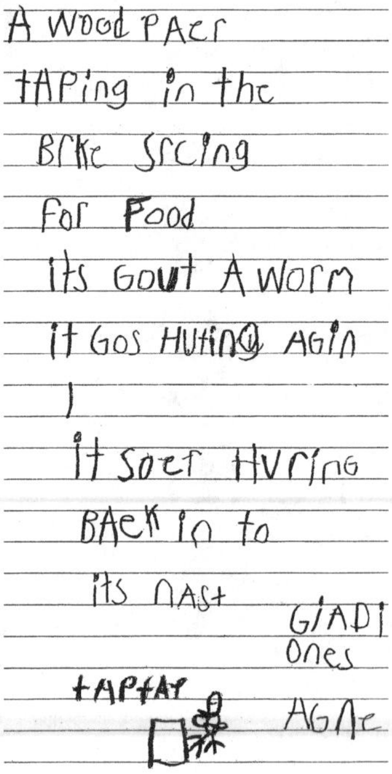

A wood paer
taping in the
brke srcing
for food
its gout a worm
it gos hufing agin
it soer hvring
bak in to
its nast
taptay
giadi ones
agne

A wood pecker
tapping in the
bark searching
for food
it's got a worm
it goes hunting again
it soars hovering
back into
its nest
tap
tap
gliding
once
again

FIGURE 6.2 Forrest writes poem about birds.

envision new possibilities for their writing—and we mean *writing* as a verb and a noun. Studies of the various aspects of the process of writing help children go about their writing work (writing as a verb) in new ways, and studies of the products of writing (writing as a noun) help children realize new possibilities in the actual texts they compose.

What Is a Unit of Study?

In the last chapter we took a close look at how whole-class teaching happens in the writing workshop and at the kinds of things we teach in these lessons. To understand units of study, then, simply imagine an extended series of lessons like those we described, happening over a period of days and weeks, with all of the lessons focused on some big topic of interest to people who write. *Some big topic of interest to people who write.* Here we are again, back at the importance of children seeing themselves as people who write. Units of study really make sense only in a room where everyone is up and writing and making stuff. Imagine, for example, that the strategy lesson we mentioned in the last chapter of reading a piece aloud to hear where the punctuation should go was one lesson in a whole series of lessons focused on *how writers use punctuation to make their texts interesting and effective*, a big topic of interest to people who write.

Most big topics of interest to people who write are related to either the process of writing or the products of writing, and so most units of study focus on one or the other, and some studies overlap the two. A study of any genre, for example, is actually a study of both process and product because we look at how writers go about writing the genre (process) and at the particulars of texts in the genre (product). The chart below summarizes some of the things people who write together might study:

PROCESS STUDIES	PRODUCT STUDIES
• living a writing life and getting and growing ideas for writing	• an overview of the kinds of writing that exist in the world, or a look at a specific kind
• a writer's work other than writing: research, observation, talk, and so on	• specific genre study: memoir, fiction (of all sorts), editorials, poetry, feature articles, essays, reviews (of all sorts), drama, and so forth
• an overview of the process of writing	
• revision	
• editing	

PROCESS STUDIES	PRODUCT STUDIES
• using a notebook as a tool to make writing better • how writers have peer conferences • how writers get published • studying our histories as writers • how to coauthor with another writer	• how to read like writers an see writer's craft in all kinds of texts—often with a specific focus on parts of texts such as leads, endings, voice, time, and description • how writers structure texts in powerful ways • how writers use words or sentences or paragraphs in powerful, crafty ways • how to make illustrations work with text • finding mentor authors for our writing • how writers use punctuation in powerful ways

What's interesting about a chart like this is that it is not grade-specific in any way. Six-year-olds might be interested in a writer's work other than writing (research, observation, talk, and so on), and sixteen-year-olds might be interested in the same topic. Six-year-olds and sixteen-year-olds might all be interested in poetry, punctuation, and peer conferences. The big topics of interest to writers are of interest to all writers, so an outline of a year of study might not look much different in first grade than in sixth grade. However, what's happening inside the studies and how the studies manifest themselves in children's writing will look quite different across grade levels. As students become more experienced with writing, the content around a specific topic becomes more and more sophisticated.

Why Organize Minilessons into Units of Study?

By definition, minilessons are short and very focused. If they are not organized over time under an umbrella of a bigger topic of interest to people who write, then our whole-class teaching can have a very hit-and-miss feel to it. For example, as we move about conferring, we might see that our students don't have any strategies for going back through a book they are writing and thinking about what they might do to make the writing more engaging. We might also notice that several of them are trying to write about content area topics they know a lot about, but they are not able to envision many different ways of going about that. We may notice that many of them aren't using their illustrations to enhance the meaning of the written words in their books and that quite a few others don't know much about good leads because they start everything by saying some version of "This is going to be about. . . ." And then, there is a whole group of students who are trying to write poetry but seem to think that rhyming is all there is to it.

We see all these issues in the children's writing, and the question is, is this five days of teaching—one minilesson each on revision, non-fiction, thoughtful illustrations, leads, and line breaks in poetry—or is it five *months* of teaching? If our answer is five days, then not one of these lessons by itself will have a chance to have much depth and really push children's thinking in significant ways. We may think, "Well, of course I'll have to come back and teach other lessons about revision and leads along the way." And of course we would have to do this if we only taught a single lesson at a time on any of these five writing issues.

But why not, instead, organize a whole series of lessons, two or three or even four weeks' worth, and study just one of these issues, say, how to make illustrations work better with the written text? The issue is one that is big enough to push the thinking of lots of different writers in lots of different developmental stages doing lots of different kinds of writing work. The luxury of deep engagement that comes from staying with a single topic over time and coming at it from a variety of angles in different lessons, is what a unit of study is all about in a writing work-shop. Staying with something in our teaching helps it—whatever the writing topic is—become bigger in children's thinking and more likely to impact their work in significant ways, as it did with Forrest and his poetry. We certainly organize curriculum in other content areas this way; we study *something* and we stay with that something for a while in our teaching.

To summarize, then, a unit of study is a series of minilessons, focused on a big topic of interest to writers, that we teach over a pe-riod of time in the writing workshop. As we think about organizing the minilessons that launch each day's workshop in this way, it's im-portant to remember that these lessons are not the only teaching of writing children are exposed during the day. Remember that, as we discussed at length in Chapter 3, our youngest writers must have op-portunities to be learning about how language works—particularly the mechanics of it all—all day long. Writing workshop is the time each day when they get to put all that learning to work and use it to do what writers actually do. This is why we focus all the whole-class teaching in the workshop on big topics of interest to *writers*: we are nurturing those identities that come to be because writing is something children do every single day.

How Do We Decide Which Units to Teach?

How do we know what big topics are of interest to writers? How do we make a chart like the one on pages 105–106 with a summary of such topics? We know this and can make a chart like this because we pull from a deep knowledge base about writing that we have developed from the existing professional literature in writing. *What a Writer Needs*, as Ralph Fletcher so aptly named one of his best books on writing, is not a mystery. The kinds of issues writers face as they write in different genres are well documented, and, as teachers of writing, we read widely to help us know what these issues are, to help us know what writers need. What is not so well documented, perhaps, is what the issues writers face are like when they are faced by five- and six- and seven-year-olds. We don't believe the issues are different; we simply believe we need to understand them developmentally. Understanding this is the real challenge of teaching our youngest writers.

The question is, then, out of all the big topics of interest to people who write, how do we decide during the school year which of these topics to address with units of study with any particular group of students? We find the guidance to make this decision each year in a number of different places:

- our vision for how we want students to *be* as writers at the end of the year
- our state and local curriculum guides
- our experience working with students in previous writing workshops
- our observation and assessment of students working in *this* writing workshop
- our own passions and interests as teachers

Let's take each one of these now and think them through a little.

Our Vision for How We Want Students to *Be* as Writers at the End of the Year

We begin by thinking carefully about what we are hoping will come of all this writing and study during the year. We ask ourselves, "After a year of writing every single day in my classroom, what kind of writers do I hope these children will become?" All our teaching, really, evolves out of our answer to this question, so it's important that we spend time really thinking about it. We want our units of study to nurture these ways of being we hope to see in the children we teach.

We know that these ways of being develop over time, so we have answered that question in this way:

OVER TIME, WE HOPE TO SEE CHILDREN DEVELOPING . . .

- a sense of self as writers, as well as personal writing processes that work for them
- ways of reading the world like writers, collecting ideas with variety, volume, and thoughtfulness
- a sense of thoughtful, deliberate purpose about their work as writers and a willingness to linger with those purposes
- their membership in a responsive, literate community
- ways of reading texts like writers, developing a sense of craft, genre, and form in writing
- a sense of audience and an understanding of how to prepare conventional writing to go into the world
(Ray 1999; Ray with Laminack 2001)

In many ways, these goals we have for children's development as writers serve as a benchmark for our planning. As frustrating as it seems sometimes, there is not *an answer* to the question of what exactly we should study at different grade levels. All we know for sure is that we should choose big topics of interest to people who write and that those topics should foster growth in the areas we want to develop. That's really the key. If we decide to undertake a unit of study and we can't see how it will help children envision new possibilities in one or more of these areas of development, then we probably need to rethink the value of spending time on it.

Our State and Local Curriculum Guides

Next, we take a close look at our state and local curriculum guides to see what expectations there are for our students at the end of the year. In our particular locale, many of the expectations for first graders have to do with the more mechanical aspects of writing. A few examples from the first-grade guide in the North Carolina Standard Course of Study are "apply phonics to write independently, using temporary and/or conventional spelling" and "use complete sentences to write simple texts" and "use basic capitalization and punctuation." We find that all of these are sort of "well, of course" kinds of issues. Just working closely with children who are generating text will get at these writing issues, and

CHAPTER 6
Organizing for Thoughtful Instruction
with Units of Study

109

these are also the kinds of things we address when we do our all-day-long teaching of how the language works.

All the parts of our curriculum guide (in North Carolina) that are more specific to the act of composition fit easily under one or more of our larger umbrellas of big topics of interest to writers. Two related expectations, for example, say that students should "select and use new vocabulary and language structures in both speech and writing contexts" and "use specific words to name and tell action in oral and written language." All of our craft study work, and particularly when we zoom in and study particular passages we like in texts, ends with helping students envision new possibilities for using language in interesting ways. One expectation says that students should "write and/or participate in writing by using an author's model of language and extending the model." All of our study of specific mentor authors is in the service of this goal. And of course, students are expected to "compose a variety of products," and all genre study is meant to help children see new possibilities for this.

We need to be sure to align all our planning for the year with our state and local curriculum guides, but the truth is, especially in primary grades, there often is not a lot of specificity (beyond general mechanics) in what is expected. Most primary teachers who have writing workshops realize the curriculum they need to offer children to support them writing every single day must go much deeper than these expectations suggest. The good news is, we are left with a lot of room to plan from our students' needs and interests and our own interests and still get at all the things that are expected in writing instruction at our grade level.

Our Experience Working with Students in Previous Writing Workshops

Because we have worked with lots of students in writing workshops before, we just know from experience that there are some things we will need to address with units of study during the year. Often these are studies that need to happen in the first weeks and months of school, as they represent critical understandings that we'll build from all year long. For example, one study that we often start the year with is an overview of the kinds of things writers make (really, an overview of different genres and forms) and how to make them in this room (an overview of management). Most first graders come to us without experience in a writing workshop, so this opening study is to show them what kinds of things are possible during the workshop.

A study of where writers get their ideas is another common study early in the year. Children facing a year's worth of writing for which they will have to find their own topic ideas usually need to think about where they'll get all these ideas. And always, early in the year we need a beginning study of how to read like writers and notice the craft of *how something is written* because any other product studies we choose to undertake (genre, structure, punctuation, illustrations, etc.) will require us to read like writers.

Our Observation and Assessment of Students Working in *This* Writing Workshop

As we get students up and going and making stuff in the writing workshop, we will begin to see the areas where they need help and where they might benefit from some deep study. A study of how to make illustrations work more thoughtfully with written text, for example, comes about because we see so many of the children write the words about one thing and then simply illustrate them with whatever they can best draw—hearts, rainbows, flowers. A study of peer conferring comes about because we see that many children really don't have any good strategies for helping one another with a piece that's under way. A study of poetry comes about because many of them are trying to write poems and need better visions for what poetry can be.

These examples are all ones we have experienced in Lisa's workshop. But the thing is, over time we are coming to realize that many of these same issues come up year after year. The timing of when they seem most ripe may vary, but young writers engaged in the work we ask them to do will face many similar issues. So while each year always looks somewhat different based on that class' particular needs, we don't completely reinvent the wheel every year. Most often, when we see what our students need help with in writing, we see it because it is so familiar; we've been down that road before with a different group of students.

We also realize and fully acknowledge that the smarter we make ourselves about writing, the more ways we see to nudge children forward in the work they are doing in writing. When we look at their work, we can't see what we don't know, in other words. This is why so many of us found so many of our conferences and minilessons were about editing issues when we first started teaching writing. That was all the knowledge of writing we left school with ourselves, and that's what we had to teach with. Now, because of that wonderful body of literature about writing, we know so much more and we use this to see with new eyes what children need to study.

Our Own Passions and Interests as Teachers

Finally, we think about what we're passionate about as teachers of writing. We believe that it is a gift to children when we share our passions with them unabashedly. So we ask ourselves, "What are the one or two things I must study with my students this year because I just won't be happy if we don't study them?" For Lisa, she must anchor some of her craft study in the work of Frank Asch and Eric Carle because she just loves their writing and illustrating, and she knows one genre study must be of literary nonfiction because she finds the work children do in this study so fascinating. She loves to show them how to write in engaging ways about the topics they know so much about, and she's invested a lot in a wonderful collection of this kind of writing to show her students new possibilities.

What Might a Year of Study Look Like in First Grade?

So, what might a year of study look like in first grade? We offer an answer to this question with some hesitation simply because we know it isn't *the* answer. A year of study at any grade level is built in all the ways we just outlined. But we want to show you one possible frame for a year of study just to give you an idea of what one *might* look like.

OVER THE YEAR IN A FIRST-GRADE WRITING WORKSHOP, WE MIGHT STUDY . . .

- the kinds of things writers make and how we'll make them in this room
- where writers get ideas
- how to read like writers
- how to find a writing mentor
- how to structure texts in interesting ways
- how to make illustrations work better with written text
- how to have better peer conferences
- the literary nonfiction genre
- how to use punctuation in interesting ways
- the poetry genre
- revision

That's eleven studies over nine months, with each one lasting anywhere from two to five weeks. The length of a study depends simply on how long we want to stay with the topic and how long we see the energy for the study lasting. We should note that there are typically a few down days in between studies when we "teach into trouble," as our friend Isoke Nia calls it. This means we deal with any management issues we see happening in the workshop or in the children's writing—issues that matter to our work but aren't *big enough* topics of interest to people who write to be a whole study. For example, one of the most passionate minilessons Katie ever watched Lisa teach was a down-day lesson about remembering to date stamp pieces of writing. When we go through the children's folders, knowing when they were working on something is so key to our assessment. The children had become careless about this and needed to be reminded of its importance, so Lisa planned a minilesson to address the problem.

Section 3 of this book is a resource section where we walk through the eleven units of study listed previously and detail the kinds of things we have done when we've studied these topics with our youngest writers. For another vision of what a year of study in K–2 writing workshops might look like, we recommend you find the wonderful resource put together by Lucy Calkins and an excellent group of primary teachers in New York City, *Units of Study for Primary Writing,* which is part of the Firsthand series from Heinemann.

What Are Our Goals for Units of Study?

When we think about this question, "What are our goals for units of study?" we sometimes find it easier to begin with being clear about what is *not* our goal. Coverage is not our goal. Big topics of interest to people who write are not topics we could cover even if we tried. There is no ending point where you know you have covered all students need to know about where writers get ideas, how writers read differently, or how to have better peer conferences. There aren't a set of specifics you can cover when studying poetry or illustrations or even how writers use punctuation to make their texts more effective. How could we ever say we've covered revision?

Our goal in a unit of study is *depth*, not coverage. We go into a study knowing we are going to dive down deep, swim around inside this topic, hold our breath as long as we can, then come back up for air. We don't end a study because we've come to the end. We end because we can see everyone has learned a lot, the energy for the study is beginning to wane, and it feels like it's time to move on to something else. When we decide to end a study, the children won't know everything they'll ever need to know about the topic, but they should know a whole lot more than when we started. We know that we can come back to a study later in the year and dive down into it again if we think it makes sense. And we certainly hope our students will have opportunities to study these big issues again and again as they develop as writers throughout their years in school.

We also know that, in some ways, a unit of study is never really over. Studies late in the year stand squarely on the shoulders of earlier studies. We continue to talk out of a study all year long in our minilessons and conferences, creating a sort of seamless, ongoing conversation about writing. A single minilesson is never really a single minilesson, in other words; it exists in a moment of time, but it doesn't stand alone. For example, students easily recognize the structures of texts in a study of literary nonfiction in February because of the deep study they did with structure in November. Punctuation—and sometimes the lack thereof—is very interesting to the children during a study of poetry late in the year because of the attention they gave to those wonderful marks earlier in the year as they learned to read like writers.

During a study and long after the study is over—the rest of the year, really—we expect children to be writing under the influence of the study. *Writing under the influence* means that we can see the content of the study manifesting itself in the children's writing. We have two main expectations for writing under the influence of every unit of study we undertake. The first is that the studies will make children more articulate about what they are doing when they write. We want our studies to give them language to talk about both the process of their work (how the writing came to be) and the products of their work (the actual texts they create). The second expectation is that the quality of the writing they do will get better and better the more we study. We do care a great deal about products and we expect our teaching to help raise the quality level of what children are able to produce.

The Nature of Process and Product Studies

Let's look now at an overview of the somewhat predictable nature of all process and product studies. We find it very helpful to think in these ways about units of study because once we get a grasp on the feel of a process or product study, any new area of study we might want to undertake seems much more doable to us.

Process Studies

In studies of process, we know we will ground most of our teaching in what professional writers have to say about how they get their writing done, in our own writing experience, and in talk around how the children are doing their writing. We usually go into these studies with some specific strategies and understandings we want to teach, and we have some idea of the resources we'll use to teach them, but there isn't a lot of scope and sequence to process studies. We just have to choose somewhere to start and keep moving the study forward. That's the nature of this kind of study. We know that things we hadn't anticipated will come up along the way and will become important pieces in the larger whole of the study. We have learned to embrace the uncertain grasp we have on where a process study might actually lead us before it's over.

Product Studies

With any product study, there are very predictable ways the whole-class teaching will go. We always begin these studies with a stack of texts, usually picture books for our youngest writers, that are full with potential for the kind of thing we are studying. As teachers, we gather most of these before the study begins, knowing we (and our students) may find others along the way as the study progresses. Once we have the stack of texts we need and we launch the study, we'll do some predictable work with what we have:

Immersion:	We spend time reading and getting to know the texts we'll study (if we don't know them already). We read with the expectation that we are going to learn something from these books, and we've established what that something is at the outset of the study.
Close study:	We revisit these texts and frame our talk with the question, "What do we notice about how these texts are written?" We ask this question in a specific way depending on what we are studying.
Articulating our learning:	We use specific language to say what we now know about writing from this close study. We record it somehow, often on a class chart. We envision using what we know in our own writing.
Writing under the influence:	This is perfectly legal, even for children! We finish at least one piece of writing (and often several) that shows the influence of the study in the writing.

While this work is predictable, it's not clearly linear. Sometimes we find ourselves, especially later in the year, engaging in close study right off the bat. We can't help ourselves—we notice things we want to talk about right away. Engaging in close study and articulating our learning are almost always happening together—one leads right to the other—and writing under the influence, especially with our youngest writers, happens throughout the study, not just at the end.

One thing we find comforting in understanding these predictable ways of teaching, especially for product studies, is the knowledge that we can launch into a study with our students even when we don't know a lot about a specific area. This has been good news for us many times, and most recently with our study of illustrations. We launched into this study without realistically anticipating all the good, solid content we'd generate with the children. We didn't really know what would come of it, but we've come to trust good writers enough, and to trust our students to notice things enough, that we don't worry about knowing the content up front. We know the close study will generate a chart full of things to know about writing when we're finished.

Genre Study: A Marriage of Process and Product Study

A genre study is a close look at a particular kind of writing. We undertake these studies with our youngest writers to help them broaden their understandings of the potential of different kinds of writing in the world. As we said earlier in the chapter, a genre study is a marriage of process and product study because we look at how writers go about writing the genre (process) and at the particulars of texts in the genre (product). We go into a genre study making it very clear to the children that they will be expected to finish at least one piece of writing in the genre we are studying. We show them our stack of books we'll be studying in the genre and we tell them, "We are all going to make a book that could go into this stack. We are going to make this *kind* of book."

Any genre study begins with immersing students in reading (or reading to them) a stack of examples we've collected, much as we'll do with any product study. We are careful to choose examples that will show our students a good variety of possibilities for their own writing in that genre. As we read through this stack together, we are thinking from two angles: process and product. We'll ask these kinds of questions for each angle:

PROCESS

- *What are these books about?* This question helps us get at the topic potential in this genre.

- *How do we think the authors got the ideas for these books?* This question helps us think about how we might choose a topic for this genre.

PROCESS

- *What do we imagine the authors had to do to write these books?* This question helps us think about what work (if any) writers have to do *other than writing* for different genres—research, observation, interviews, and so on.

PRODUCT

- *What are the characteristics of this kind of writing? What makes it different from other kinds of writing?* These questions help us begin to identify the genre more specifically as a certain kind of writing.

- *What are some different ways writers approach the writing of this genre? What do we notice about the craft of the writing in these books?* These questions help us find possibilities for how to write well in this genre.

These questions will guide us as we study the genre and begin to think about writing our own books that can go into the stack of books we are studying. As with any process study, we'll bring in authors' voices from wherever we can find them to tell us things about how they write in these genres. In a genre study of literary nonfiction, for example, we might listen as Seymour Simon tells us, "I love finding out everything I can about a subject such as gorillas or hurricanes or black holes in space. For me, the best part of writing science books is doing the research on these fascinating subjects" (in Marcus' *Author Talk* 2000, 96). This quote will help the children understand that one of the potentials of this genre is that it affords you an opportunity to spend time researching a topic you know and love. Or during the poetry study, we might listen as Lee Bennett Hopkins tells us, "A poem usually starts with an image, something I've seen on a walk—a nest of young pigeons, for instance" (Marcus 2000, 32). This quote would help the children understand that we need to, well, walk differently! We need to walk around like poets. Our charts will fill with specific understandings, strategies, and techniques we are generating from our close study of both the process and the products of the genre.

In genre study with older and more experienced writers, we often ask them to delay starting drafts of their required pieces in the genre until we are nearing the end of the study. Along the way, we have them use their writers' notebooks to try things out that we're learning. We have decided not to do this with our youngest writers because they don't write fast enough to just try things out in a notebook, and we believe that holding off and storing up a vision for writing they'll *eventually* do is just not developmentally appropriate for them. Instead, we encourage them to go ahead and start writing in the genre as soon as they'd like. Many of the children will start right away and will complete several pieces in the genre—sometimes about the same topic, sometimes about different topics—during the study. And then there usually are a few we have to remind as the study nears its end that they need to work on beginning and finishing a piece in this genre.

At the end of a genre study, we expect the children to be able to talk about what they've written as an example of the genre and we will listen for this in our assessment of their writing. We'll listen, for example, for them to explain how they have included facts in their nonfiction or how their line breaks work in poetry. We will also expect them to use some of the techniques we have seen other writers of this genre use in the books we've studied, and we hope the children will be able to explain some of these techniques. In their actual texts, we'll look for evidence that shows what they've learned in the study, some of which we know they won't yet be able to articulate.

"So, what should we study next in writing?" is a question we live with all the time as teachers of writing. We know we want to study something that will raise the level of the writing work in the room, so we try to stay very close to that work day by day as we figure out how to answer this question again and again throughout the year.

CHAPTER 7

Assessment

Learning All We Can About the Authors

One morning Katie comes across Riley wandering about the room during writing workshop. He has a serious look on his face. "What are you doing?" she asks him.

"I've got to find some black paper," he says.

"Black paper?"

"For the nighttime parts. Me and Taylor are doing a book about sleeping over on our camping trip and I want to do the nighttime parts on black paper."

Black paper. For the nighttime parts. Katie writes it down in her notes and tabs it so she'll be sure to share it with Lisa.

As we have worked with young children over time, we have come to see interactions like this one with Riley as having incredibly important assessment potential. We've learned that to assess the writing work of young children, we've got to be right out there in the messy, real, wonderful middle of all their work. Katie probably expected she had discovered Riley in a morning avoidance mode, taking a walk about the room instead of writing. Instead, she found him in the midst of carrying out a decision about his writing, the most important place we believe we can find children in a writing workshop.

Catching Them in the Act

As we have discussed throughout this book, children go out to write each day in a room filled with ideas for things they might try in their writing or ways they might go about their work. The purpose of our whole-class teaching, in fact, is to plant these ideas and help the children see them as real possibilities. And even though we don't assign children specific things to do or try in their writing, we make it very clear that we expect them to try things on their own. It is not uncommon for Lisa to dismiss the children from the day's minilesson with this kind of reminder: "I want to see you all trying things today. Think about what we've been learning and try some of it in your writing."

It follows, then, that one of the main purposes of our assessment is to find evidence of the children using these ideas to make decisions about their writing work each day, catching them in the act, if you will. This is why it was a big deal to Katie that Riley was so purposefully looking for black paper. It showed he was being decisive about *how* he was doing his writing, and this is incredibly important assessment data for us. Perhaps our most important goal for children at the end of first grade is that they will come to see writing as a continuous process of decision making. We want them to learn that as authors, they are in charge of how a piece of writing comes to be.

Now, that may sound like just a cute, kid-friendly way to approach writing—"As authors, you are in charge." But we don't see it that way. We believe that decisiveness is one of the defining characteristics of truly accomplished writers. We believe that accomplished writers know a lot about how language works, a lot about the potentials of different genres and forms of writing, a lot about how to make the parts of a text work together structurally. And we believe that accomplished writers use all this knowledge to make decisions, all along the way, that impact how a text comes to be. So when we see a six-year-old making a very specific, intentional decision about how he wants his writing to be, we know this is an important marker in his becoming an accomplished writer.

In addition to this, catching children in the act of trying things on their own is our only true way of knowing whether they are getting it— the *it* being all the writing curriculum we are offering up as possibilities in our teaching. It is one thing to see that a child can do something if we ask him to do it; it is quite another entirely to see him decide to do it on his own. For example, during a study of peer conferences, we might have all the children pair up and have conferences where they talk through a piece to make the ideas bigger. As they do this, we can watch and observe and learn some things about what they know about this kind of interaction. But it's not until we actually see them seek out a peer for a conference on their own for just this reason—to make their ideas bigger—that we know they have truly internalized this way of working through the process. Same thing with text possibilities. We may have everyone sit on the carpet and think of a stronger verb for some sentence in his or her writing and be quite happy when each child finds one, but we need to catch them in the act of using this technique on their own, away from us, to really know they've internalized the work of a strong verb.

Now, this doesn't mean that we don't often ask children to do very specific things just like this. We do, in both minilessons and writing conferences, and we're there to offer help as they do them. We may help some of them again and again with some things. But as teachers, we live for those moments when we see children do them all on their own. That's when we know, for sure, that our teaching is taking hold. Catching them in the act of trying something on their own is at the heart of all our assessment.

In this chapter we want to consider four ways of angling assessment to help us capture important insights about what children are learning about writing from our teaching and from their everyday engagement with it. We'll think about assessment as

- looking closely at individual pieces of writing
- watching and listening as children are engaged in the process
- asking children to be articulate
- looking across the work of a single child over time

With each angle, we'll list some lines of thinking (in the form of questions) that we've found helpful in understanding children's work. We should note that we don't go down these lists of questions and tick off an answer to each one. These are simply the kinds of things we're thinking about as we're continuously assessing what's happening with children and their writing.

Looking Closely at Individual Pieces of Writing

When we look at a finished piece of writing, the main assessment question that guides us is, "What does this piece of writing show me this child knows about writing?" It's that simple, and it's that complex. As an example, let's look at a piece titled *I Am the Snake*, written by Cauley in late winter during our study of literary nonfiction (see Figure 7.1). Let's look at it closely and try naming all the things we see he knows about writing. And with this first naming, let's look only at what he knows *beyond* the simple mechanics of writing—left-to-right orientation, spacing between words, good knowledge of spelling patterns, and so forth. What does he know in addition to that kind of thing? What does he know about crafting a piece of literature?

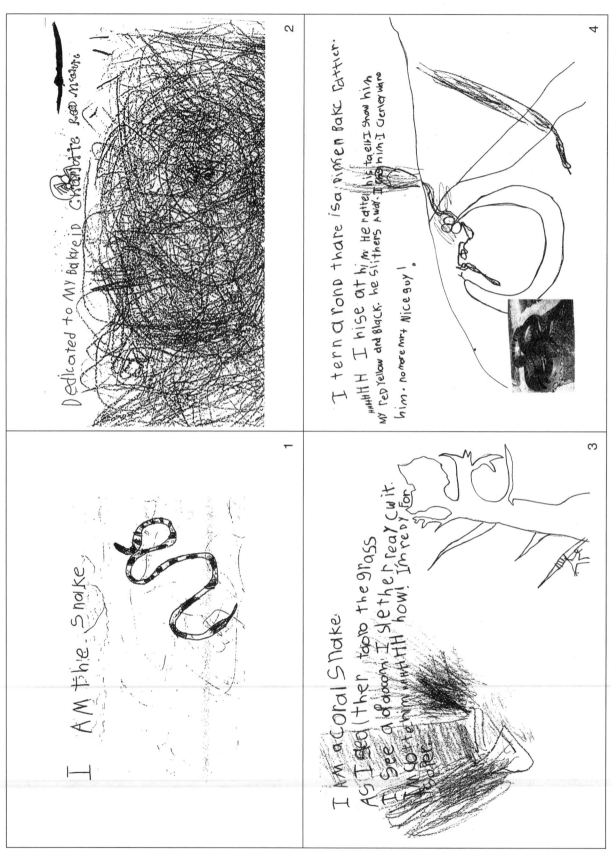

FIGURE 7.1 Cauley's *I Am the Snake* book. (3) I am a coral snake. As I slither through the grass, I see an opposum. I slither really quiet. I'm close to him. HHHH Now! I'm ready for supper. (4) I turn around. There is a diamondback rattler. HHHH I hiss at him. He rattles his tail. I show him my red, yellow, and black. He slithers away. I chase him. I clearly warned him. No more Mr. Nice Guy!

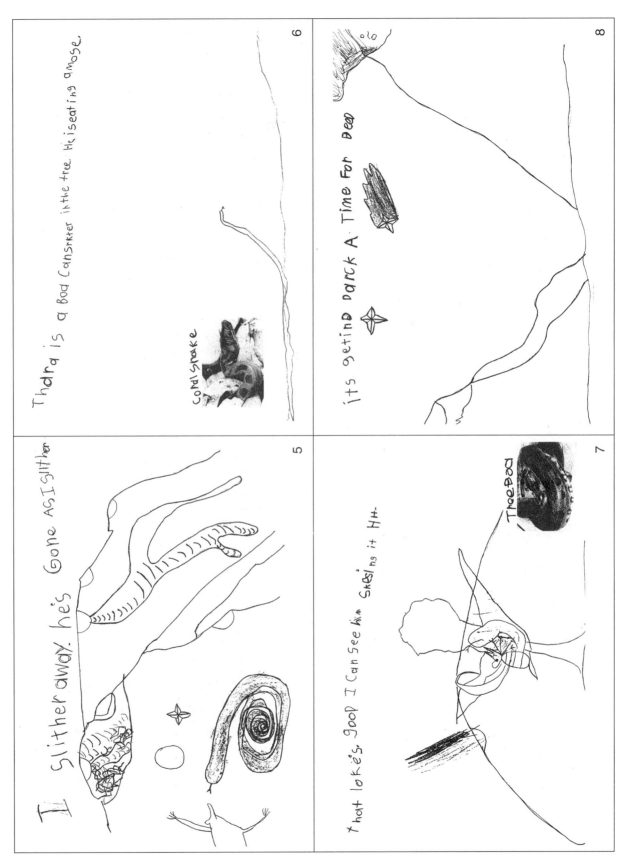

FIGURE 7.1 *continued* (5) I slither away. He's gone as I slither. (6) There is a boa constrictor in the tree. He is eating a mouse. (7) That looks good. I can see him squeezing it. HHH (8) It's getting dark and time for bed.

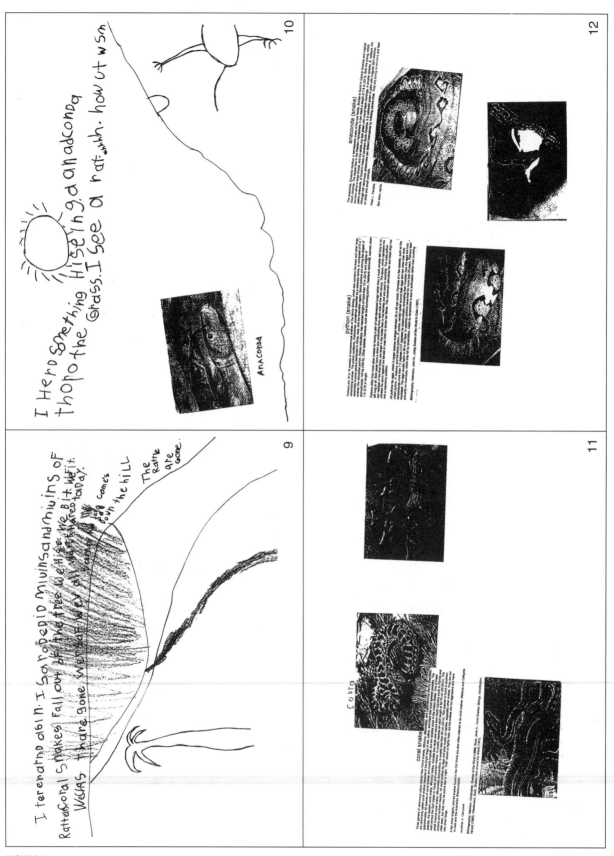

FIGURE 7.1 *continued* (9) I turn around again. I'm surrounded. Millions and millions of rattlers coral snakes fall out of the tree. We hiss. We bite. We fight. We chase. They're gone. We've all worked hard today. Scorching hot lava comes down the hill. The rattlers are gone. (10) I heard something hissing. An anaconda through the grass. I see a rat. HHH How it was. Pages 11 and 12 have facts about snakes that Cauley has printed from the computer.

Our list looks like this. Cauley knows

- One kind of text a writer can make is a picture book.
- Books of this kind often have dedications (Charlotte Reed McClure was Cauley's pet spider) (p. 2).
- Books of this kind can have a mix of fact and story (a sense of genre).
- Pictures in a text like this are often labeled (pp. 6, 7, 10).
- Facts in a text like this are often placed at the end and they relate to what happened in the story line.
- One way to approach a topic like this (snakes) is to use first-person narration and give your topic a voice.
- With first-person narration, we might get some inside thinking from our narrator (p. 7, "that looks good").
- A writer can create a spelling to match a sound he wants heard in his writing ("hhhh . . .").
- A story like this can be written in present tense as if it is happening as you're reading it.
- A text can be written to follow the movement of something, in this case, the snake.
- Illustrations can add more detail to words on the page (p. 7).
- A writer can bring the playfulness of oral language into writing (p. 4, "No more Mr. Nice Guy").
- A series of very short sentences with strong verbs can show dramatic action (pp. 4, 9).
- The feeling of some time period ending (in this case, the end of a day) can bring a sense of closure to a text (p. 8).
- An illustration can run (in this case literally!) off the edge of the page (p. 10).
- The way the print goes down on the page can be manipulated to make meaning (p. 9, "hot lava comes down the hill").

Now, when we (Lisa and Katie) make this list, we have two distinct advantages over anyone else making this list. First, we know the teaching that is feeding the piece. Many of the things we notice Cauley doing strike us because we know they're things the class talked about in different studies during the year. So much of what we're able to see in children's writing grows as our own knowledge base for teaching grows and we're feeding them more and more possibilities. In other words, the more we teach them, the more we see them trying things in their writing. We're not at all surprised to see Cauley trying those two series of short, action-packed sentences when the snakes start fighting. Using short sentences to show dramatic action is something we've seen other writers do in their books and so the children know that as a very real possibility for their writing.

The second advantage we have, of course, is that we know Cauley, so we are impressed with some things because of that knowledge. For example, that he puts in the language "No more Mr. Nice Guy" really matters to us because Cauley is one of those children who surprises us again and again with the things he *says*, and we have been wanting him to do that more with the things he *writes*. We consider his using that language an important marker in his growing ease with language in writing.

When looking at a piece of writing to see what the child knows about crafting a piece of literature, there are some predictable lines of thinking guiding our assessment:

- Do I see any evidence in this piece that the child is trying writing ideas we've discussed in minilessons or share time?
- Does the piece show a strong sense of form and genre? If so, in what way?
- Does the piece show a strong sense of structure?
- Has the child used an interesting approach to the writing?
- Has the child tried any interesting language work in the writing?
- If the piece is illustrated, how well do the illustrations enhance the meaning of the written words?

Now, let's look at his piece just in terms of the mechanics of the language. Before we look at a child's piece in this way, we need to know how much specific attention to mechanics (outside of drafting) the child has done. In other words, is this writing the result of getting it down the first time—which often includes some editing—or is it the result of a careful revisiting during which the child has tried to edit everything he can find that he missed that first time through? We find it helpful during the year to look at children's writing in both stages because it helps us better understand their individual processes. And of course, as we mentioned in Chapter 4, until children have developed some essential understandings that will help them edit, we won't expect them to revisit and change much anyway.

Also, as we look at any mechanics, we must keep in mind what is developmentally appropriate for children this age. We are not going to be concerned with more sophisticated language issues such as agreement between subjects and verbs or pronouns and antecedents, consistency of verb tenses, subtle comma uses, and the like until children are very much in control of more basic conventions such as word spacing, end punctuation, and good spelling generalizations. And for many of them, being very much in control of basic conventions won't happen while they are in first grade.

The *I Am the Snake* piece in Figure 7.1 has not gone through a careful once-over by Cauley for editing, though he is a child who tends to make some editing changes as he goes. The piece, then, is a good example of how much Cauley is controlling language in the "getting it down the first time" stage of writing. Our key lines of thinking when we look at a piece of writing in this way are

- What mechanical issues do we see this child controlling with some consistency?
- What do we think he could find (because he has the understandings to help him) in editing if he set his mind to it?
- What do we see that he might need some explicit teaching to help him get under control?
- How's he doing with spelling?

When we look at Cauley's piece with these questions guiding us, we see several things. First, we see that he has a very good sense of complete sentence structure. His use of end punctuation to separate these sentences is a little inconsistent, though it's there when it matters most ("We hiss. We bite. We fight. We chase. They're gone."). He also shows some variety in end punctuation, using an exclamation mark in some very smart places and not overusing it in a piece that has the potential for that because of all the dramatic action. All in all, Cauley certainly seems to have the necessary understandings to go back and edit now for end punctuation (and the accompanying capitalization), so this piece tells us it's time to nudge him to do that.

As for other punctuation, he is using the apostrophe and shows he has a fairly good developing sense of how it can be used to contract words—*I'm, he's*. He overgeneralizes this some, as with *loke's* (*looks*) and *come's*, and leaves it out completely in "*its* getting dark." It would be wise for us to teach into this convention and offer Cauley some more direct instruction on how this mark works since he is clearly trying to understand its use.

The only other thing we would likely think about in terms of mechanics other than spelling is word spacing. Cauley clearly understands that words have spaces between them, but he's inconsistent in his spacing. We might need to observe him writing to figure out why this inconsistency is happening. Is it because he gets very into the idea of what he's writing and writes more quickly? Is it because he's trying to squeeze a lot into a little space? We might ask him what he thinks about why this happens. Whatever the explanation, this is something we'd ask Cauley to really keep in mind on his next piece of writing, rather than something we'd have him edit for here, since he'd have to completely rewrite the problematic pages to change the spacing on them.

Finally, how's he doing with spelling? The piece clearly shows us he's not afraid to spell, as there are lots of examples of challenging spellings and not all of them are names of snakes. He also uses rich vocabulary such as *surrounded, squeezing, slither,* and *scorching.* Nice choices for a *ssss*nake piece, huh?

Cauley seems to be using a variety of strategies to spell unfamiliar words. Sometimes he is clearly using sound, as in his spelling of *cwit* (*quiet*). Sometimes he is using knowledge of familiar word patterns, as he shows when he doubles the *l* in his spelling of *taell* (tail). He uses his knowledge of different endings (*-ing, -ly*) for several spellings, though the impact on other letters when these endings are added is something he still is working out in his understanding. And he is most certainly using his visual memory to spell, something very obvious in the spelling of the different snake names.

His control of high-frequency words is especially good, though it may not appear to be at first glance. If we do a quick index of control (Laminack and Wood 1996, 48–49) on the piece, we see that there are 179 total words in what he's written (counting all but the last page, with the Internet information on it). Of these 179 total words, 105 of them are different words (the others are repetitions; *I* is used 16 times, for instance), and of these 105 different words, 62 are spelled conventionally at least once (3 of them are spelled conventionally in one instance and not so in another). What do these numbers mean? They mean that Cauley is controlling the spelling of 59 percent of the words he's using in this piece, most of them high-frequency words. Not bad for a beginning writer who is writing with this rich complexity of vocabulary. And remember, this piece is basically as he wrote it the first time. If we nudged Cauley to spend a little time going over his spellings carefully, he might raise that index of control by as much as 5 or 10 percent.

Watching and Listening as Children Are Engaged in the Process

Looking closely at a piece of finished writing can certainly tell us a lot about what children know, but watching and listening to them as they write can help us capture so much more insight and information, especially in terms of understanding their processes. You may remember that in Chapter 4 we explained that we needed to get them using some process to write before we would know what to teach them about process. Well, assessment is really the key to this making any teaching sense at all. So much of what we understand they *need* as writers comes from watching them as they actually do the writing.

Take Levi, for example. One morning in late spring we watched Levi compose three separate poems—one about getting ready in the mornings, one about playing with his sister, and one about an Easter egg hunt—and for each one, he followed the same methodical process. He first drew a line to separate a single page of paper. Then he sketched a picture at the bottom of the page (an alarm clock, a bubble-blowing gun, and an Easter basket). Then, almost seamlessly, he moved to the top of the page and wrote each poem. Three times he did this in one morning.

We noted this process and realized as we watched Levi that he was writing with much more fluency than we had ever seen. He was also still very reliant on his drawing to help him frame his thinking before writing. This was something we had nudged many of the children away from because we felt they were ready to let their writing lead their thinking more. Observing Levi that morning helped us understand that he was growing in one very important way—he was developing fluency—but that his process for that needed to be different than the one many of the children were using. If we hadn't watched Levi and learned this about him as a writer, we might have forced some expectations on him that were not only inappropriate, they were unnecessary. In fact, we expect Levi may grow to be a very experienced, accomplished writer someday and still use sketching as a way to frame his thinking because he responds so naturally to his visual sense of the world.

We also need to be watching children as they write to see if our teaching about process is taking hold in their work. Are they using the understandings and strategies we're offering them about process to raise the level of their work? This is something we almost surely wouldn't know if we didn't listen and watch as children were writing. Sometimes it is weeks and even months later before we see evidence of our teaching about process taking hold, but actually we believe the evidence is much stronger when we do it see it much later.

Take, for example, a peer conference we overheard where Clay and Tayler were helping Helena with her book *How My Dog Gets Dirty*. During the conference, Clay said to Helena, rather pleadingly, "We're not saying that your title is bad, we're just saying there could be better ones out there." In this simple little comment, we see the tracks of earlier teaching. That they are addressing her rather label-like title in their conference harkens back to several discussions about titles that were part of a study of how to read like writers much earlier in the year. And that Clay seems very conscious of the fact that he needs to be supportive of the writer, that he knows exploring other options doesn't mean the writer has done something bad, seems to be talk directly out of our study of peer conferring that occurred a few weeks before this conference took place.

And of course, so much of what we need to know about how children get the words down on the page we'll learn by watching them as they write. So much of our best teaching help in writing conferences will come from first observing and listening and then helping the children refine what we see them doing. As we watch a young writer (let's say she's a girl), we'll use these overlapping lines of thinking to help us understand the process she is using for writing:

- How quickly does she generate spellings? Is this different for high-frequency words versus unfamiliar words?

- Does she seem fearless as a speller, or does she stay with safe words most of the time?

- How much is she sounding out as she spells? What other strategies do we see her using?

- Does she talk something out before she writes it?

- Does she embed lots of thinking about what she'll write next, or does the text seem to be already written inside her head?

- Does she interact with other children as she writes?

- Does drawing seem to be an integral part of her thinking process for the writing, or something she does as an addition to the writing or not at all?

- If there is punctuation in the piece, how is it going in? Does she insert it as she goes, or does she insert it when she rereads? Some of both?

- Does she stop and reread what she's written? If so, what seems to be the purpose of this? Is she trying to get the meaning and flow of the text going again? Does she self-correct at all when (if) she rereads? If so, what kinds of things is she self-correcting for?

- Does she ever change something that is clearly a matter of revision (to make the writing better) and not of editing? If so, what's her process for doing this?

- How does she get started on a new piece of writing? What's the first thing she does?

- How does she start working on a piece that's already under way? What's the first thing she does when she comes back to it?

- How does she seem to know she's finished? What does she do when she thinks she's finished?

- When she reads what she's written, does she read it so it sounds like a piece of literature?

- Does she seem to find what she has written to be engaging in any way? Does she laugh or sigh at her own words? Does she share the piece spontaneously with other children?

Asking Children to Be Articulate

After just a few weeks of school, children in Lisa's writing workshop come to understand that they will be asked, again and again, to respond to the request, "Tell me about what you are working on." Every writing conference that interrupts their work—and that's most writing conferences—begins with some version of this question. We ask the question for two reasons tied to assessment.

First, we ask it because sometimes children give us insightful information that helps us understand their work. They tell us things we simply would never know if we didn't ask. For example, one morning when we came upon Meagan working on a book in which flowers were arguing over which of them was prettiest, she explained to us that she had gotten the idea for this book from a book Kayla had written in which tigers were fighting over who was the best. The two books were distinct enough that we probably wouldn't have guessed Meagan had gotten the idea from Kayla, but once she told us this, it was very important assessment information for us. Meagan was a writer willing and able to be influenced by other writers whose work she admired.

The second reason we ask this question again and again is because it is our best assessment of whether children are using the language of our teaching to help them become articulate about their writing. One of the main goals we have for our teaching of writing is that it will help children speak a new language—the language of writers—and that in turn, this new language will help them imagine new possibilities. For example, on another morning when Meagan and Kayla seemed to be working together, they explained to us that they were working on a sequel to their earlier book about some girls going to the river and finding some treasure. A *sequel*. The word itself (and their understanding of it, of course) helped these young writers imagine new possibilities. Our ears perk up any time we hear a child using the language of our teaching to explain their writing work to us.

We have another important reason for asking children to explain to us what they are doing when they write, but this reason is more instructional. We believe that being asked again and again to explain their writing teaches them to think about how and why they are writing things in certain ways. *Why* and *how* questions often follow in conferences, and we don't worry in those first few months that they don't have much to say, because over time we see that children get better and better at articulating answers for us. We just have to keep asking them.

In addition to asking children to explain what they are working on when we interrupt them, we also frequently ask them to walk us through a piece of writing and talk to us about how they've written it. "Tell me about each page and what you were thinking," we say, and again, we know that at first they don't have much to say in response, but over time they'll come to see themselves as people who should be able to answer that question, and they'll grab hold of their decision making more specifically. In fact, we believe that their anticipation of being asked that question often leads them to make more interesting decisions about how they will write something. This is especially true when they realize that most often we use share time to look at interesting decisions children have made as they write their books.

In any product study, we almost always ask children to write at least one piece that shows the influence of the study—for example, in a genre study, everyone must write at least one piece in that genre; in a study of structure, children must write at least one piece where we can see they have carefully chosen a text structure; in a study of punctuation, we must see a piece that shows specific punctuation decisions. Most often in our assessments for these studies, we simply have children walk us through these pieces and talk to us about the decisions they've made. With most students, we expect to see an intricate mix of writing moves about which they are very articulate and writing moves we know they know but aren't yet able to explain.

Take Cauley's *I Am the Snake* piece, for example. While there is a lot he can explain about what's happening in this book, he doesn't ex-

FIGURE 7.2 Lisa and Sadie talk about how Sadie has written her book.

plain all of it when we ask him about it. The series of short sentences with strong verbs, for instance, was not something he articulated on his own. We know he knows this way of making language work, and we know we've used specific language (*short sentences, strong verbs, strong feel of action*) to talk about it as a class when we've seen it in books. But these words just aren't comfortable for him yet; after all, writing workshop is probably the only time and place where he and his classmates hear language used in this way. Most of us just don't have opportunities to use words like "verb" in our everyday lives! Nonetheless, the writing move he's made is fairly hard to explain without these words. When we see that a child very obviously knows something like this about writing but isn't able to articulate it, we often take the opportunity to use the language again and name for him what we see him doing.

As children talk to us about their writing, there are just a few lines of thinking we follow as we listen:

- Do I hear in this child's responses that he is being decisive as he writes?

- What language is this child using to talk about writing? Is any of it the language of my teaching?

- What do I see that he knows but doesn't seem able to explain? Does it make sense to point this out to him? If so, what language would he need to explain it? Is it language we've used before?

Looking Across the Work of a Single Child Over Time

So much of what we see in a child's work, and particularly so much of what we do and say in response to a child's work, has to do with understanding that work in a historical context. Because we think a lot about a child's work across the year, we know if we are seeing something for the first time or the one hundredth time, what is safe and what is a risky stretch. We know what's becoming automatic, what's still experimental, and what's not even happened yet. Things strike us in a child's work because they are so different. Or because they are so familiar. As we work alongside children, one question is always on the edge of our thinking: "How does what I'm seeing here fit with what I already know about this child?"

Take Forrest, for example. Late in the year he began working on a project that really required us to know his history as a writer to appreciate what he was doing. An observer walking in for just a day might not have been very impressed. When we asked him what he was working on, Forrest's response was, "It's a book about army men and it's going to be probably about fifty pages long." Now, wanting lots of volume in their writing as they become more fluent is very common for young children. This was the first time we had seen Forrest cross over into that "volume is everything" stage. But because we knew this child and his writing so well, there was more to it for us than just that.

With the army men book, Forrest was doing a kind of writing that was very new for him. Across the year he had stayed almost exclusively with topics he knew a lot about. He was a young man who was fascinated by and retained all sorts of interesting facts about the natural world, and so this led him to write a lot of list books, especially nonfiction ones about animals and space. Generating a lot of volume with this kind of writing was a challenge because basically he was limited by what he knew about the topic he'd chosen. The army men book, on the other hand, was completely fictional, and he was experiencing what seemed to be a real joy at making it up as he went along. He was so excited to realize that what he was writing could just go on and on. And the writing had such a different energy than the more factual books he was used to writing. It was written in present tense and the words interacted directly with the pictures, as you can see in the excerpt in Figure 7.3.

For days Forrest stayed with the book and continued to add all sorts of action. He would seek us out to tell us how many pages it was at that point and how many he thought it would be in the end. Several times we saw that he had sought out other children and was reading the

FIGURE 7.3 Some pages from Forrest's army men book. (1) Sergeant calls reinforcements. We need help. We're getting destroyed. Only three men left. Let's get out of here. (2) The tan are coming from the side. (3) The blue drops a yo-yo. It blows him to smithereens. (4) The red are getting dropped down by airplane. The blue are watching. What's this? A blue fighter jet. We're under attack.

book to them. There was a new sort of energy to his work that we understood because we understood the historical importance of this piece of writing: Forrest was doing something with writing (making a story up) that he'd never really done before. In fact, the army men book is a perfect example of a piece of writing that really mattered to us primarily because of what it represented on the time line of his writing life. If we hadn't known Forrest's history, we might have overlooked the piece altogether, or worse yet, we might have tried to redirect him into some different work that we valued more.

We believe it is critical that all our assessment happen within a historical context. We must try to understand any one moment in time as it relates to all the other moments we've shared with each child. Here are some of the lines of thinking we use to understand a child's work over time:

- What is different and new in this child's work? What's familiar? (At different times we'll ask this about all aspects of process, and about topic choice, genre, text structure, word choice, sentence structure, conventions, etc.)

- Is there variety in what the child is trying to do, or does the child seem to be doing the same thing over and over? (This question is about the writing itself, not about topic choice; a child may be writing about the same topic a lot and still be doing different kinds of writing.)

- Have any patterns evolved in this child's work that we might need to address?

- What makes sense as a logical next step in nudging this child's development?

What Happens to All This Assessment Information?

For years we've tinkered with different ways of keeping a written track of all we're learning about children as we work alongside them and assess both their products and their processes, and there's one thing we've learned for sure: we can't keep track of it *all* and still teach. All these wonderful lines of thinking we outlined in this chapter lead us to many layers of thinking about each of the children we teach, and every bit of the thinking we do about them is important to our work with them. As a matter of fact, we believe that the act of thinking deeply as we teach *is* a continual act of assessment. But to make notes about every thought we have about a child or everything we notice in that child's writing would leave us with no time to teach, no time to act on what we're assessing.

So, we have to be selective and specific about what seems most important out of all we're noticing and thinking about a child's work. How do we know what's important? What specifics do we need to be sure to be able to recall later? It's hard to pin down, but it seems to come down to just a few kinds of things that really matter:

- new areas of growth we see in a child's work
- possibilities for logical next steps in nudging a child's development
- possibilities for whole-class teaching out of a child's experience
- a record of the teaching we did in a writing conference

It helps if we have somewhere to make notes of these kinds of things during writing workshop, something we can carry around easily with us as we're working with the children, and the more organized these notes are, the better. At least we imagine this to be true; neat organization of assessment notes is not a strong suit for either of us. Be that as it may, the bottom line is we have to be able to collect all the thinking we've done about a single child so we can revisit that thinking and see the bigger assessment picture we're creating over time. We also need to select representative pieces of writing periodically and attach assessment notes to them.

We'll use our assessment (both the ongoing thinking and any written notes we've made) of each child in several ways. First and foremost, we'll use our assessment to direct our teaching. What we learn can help us make plans for future whole-class study that we see is needed, but even more importantly, ongoing assessment always helps us make good decisions about what to teach individual children in writing conferences. Our assessment can make the teaching that happens during share time each day much richer as well. We are always on the lookout for smart work we see children doing that they might share with others and in doing so broaden the pool of what's possible in the writing workshop.

Obviously, we'll need our assessment to help us provide whatever kinds of reported data are required by the systems in which we teach. In many schools, thankfully, grades for writing at the primary level are not required, only descriptions of a child's development in writing across the year. Our written assessment notes and the representative pieces that accompany them are essential in helping us evaluate this development for report cards.

A strong sense of ongoing assessment also helps us tremendously in our work with parents. We find that very often parents are not familiar with the kind of writing instruction their children are experiencing in the writing workshop, so we must be able to communicate in a very clear way all the many kinds of things their children are learning about writing. In parent conferences, Lisa spreads out representative pieces of writing and her own notes she's taken on individual children, and then she walks parents through all there is to see there. Imagine being a parent and having Cauley's piece explained to you in the way we explained it at the beginning of this chapter, with all the remarkable things he knows about writing enumerated for you one by one. In general, parents are quite supportive when we take the time to help them—in clear, articulate language—understand our teaching and see that their children are learning so much from it.

Finally, our assessment is important because it helps us maintain a celebratory attitude about our teaching. We need to know if Michaela has written her very first poem. We need to know if Josh thought about writing *dog* instead of *dalmatian* but then changed his mind and tackled the more difficult spelling. We need to know if Ashley reread an old book she'd written and decided to completely redo the ending. So often, children don't even realize they have done remarkable things in their writing. We must help them see this and then make room for celebration. After all, as Byrd Baylor taught us, we're in charge of celebrations in our classrooms. Good assessment helps us know when to party—or just give a good ole high five that feels sort of like a party!

 CHAPTER 8

Teaching Into and Out of the Work of Individual Children

Writing Conferences and Share Times

Each morning as the children leave the minilesson and go out to work on their writing, Lisa follows them and begins her daily routine of meeting with different children for writing conferences. She moves about the room as she confers, and a single writing conference usually lasts anywhere from five to ten minutes. The purpose of these conferences is to offer children individualized instruction in their writing work.

Writing conferences follow a predictable pattern. First, we assess what the child is doing at that moment in time with writing. We may quietly observe for a few moments first, and then we almost always ask the child to talk to us about what she's doing. As we're watching and listening, we're thinking about everything we already know about this child and how that fits with what she's doing now. We're trying to decide what we might help her with that would make the most sense at this time and would likely help her in the future of her writing life. Often, we see several possibilities for what we might teach, but we have to decide on just one (or two if they are closely related) for this single interaction because we don't want to overwhelm these young writers with too much teaching.

Because children are often sitting at tables with three or four others, it's not uncommon for several writers to be engaged in the talk of one conference. Sometimes we invite input from other children, sometimes they offer it unsolicited, but often we just see that they are listening in as we talk to another writer sitting near them. We embrace the listening in that they do because so often we see the impact of this kind of residual teaching. We'll see evidence that children have actually learned the content of someone else's conference and are using it in their writing.

As we are thinking about what we'll teach, we have to keep in mind the very sound advice we learned from Lucy Calkins and remember that we're supposed to teach the writer, not the writing. Sometimes we want to make the writing better with our teaching, but that's not the point. The point is to make the *writer* better.

We had to remember this as we worked with Marissa in a conference early in the year. When we approached her, Marissa showed us the book she was working on and said, "I'm finished with this." We looked at what she had on the five page spreads (see Figure 8.1).

As we looked at the book, what we saw was very familiar. Early in the year, even our most advanced writers sometimes tend to stay with safe kinds of writing. They use words that are comfortable for them, as Marissa did with *nice*, they use a lot of repetition, and they write about the same topics a lot. This was Marissa's second or third book about flowers in just a few short weeks. We knew that Marissa could do so much more with this piece of writing, but we also knew that we had been trying to establish some solid criteria in the room for being finished and that she had clearly worked to meet those criteria. Her pages were full of illustrations and writing, all of them were about the same idea, and her illustrations matched her words. When she used our teaching language, "I'm finished," to describe to us where she was with the writing, she was defining it in the context of her work exactly as we had defined it for the class.

So even though we knew Marissa could make this piece of writing better, we had to remember that this piece of writing wasn't the point. What might we teach her in this context that would make Marissa a better writer? We decided to talk to her about her topic, flowers, and how it seemed likely this was a topic she would revisit again as a writer. We helped her imagine that on her next book about flowers she might tell us even more about roses and daisies because we suspected she knew a lot more about them. We invited her to tell us more about them, and she did. We helped her envision writing this in her next book, several ideas on each page, and then we suggested that she might also become a flower detective when she was at home and study the flowers she loves so she might write about them even better.

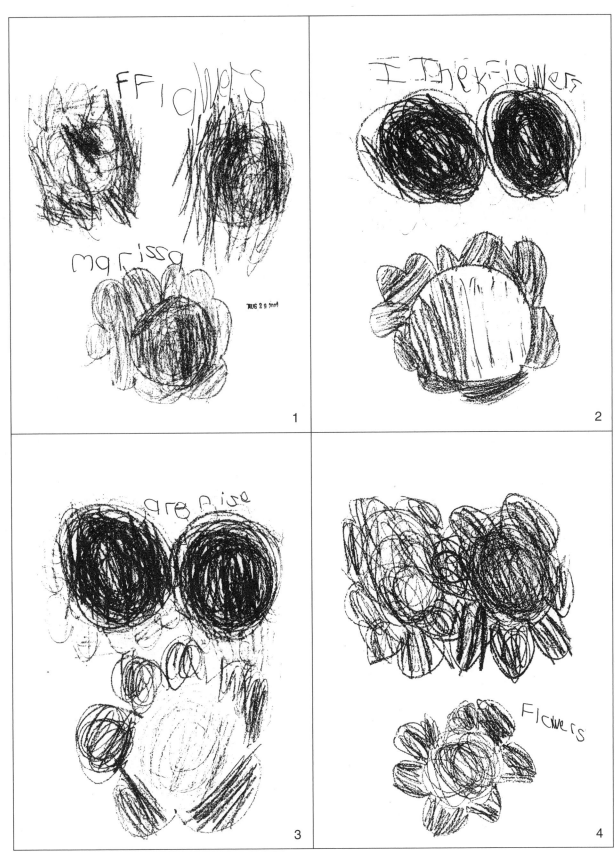

FIGURE 8.1 Marissa's finished book about flowers. (1) Flowers (2) I think flowers (3) are nice. (4) Flowers.

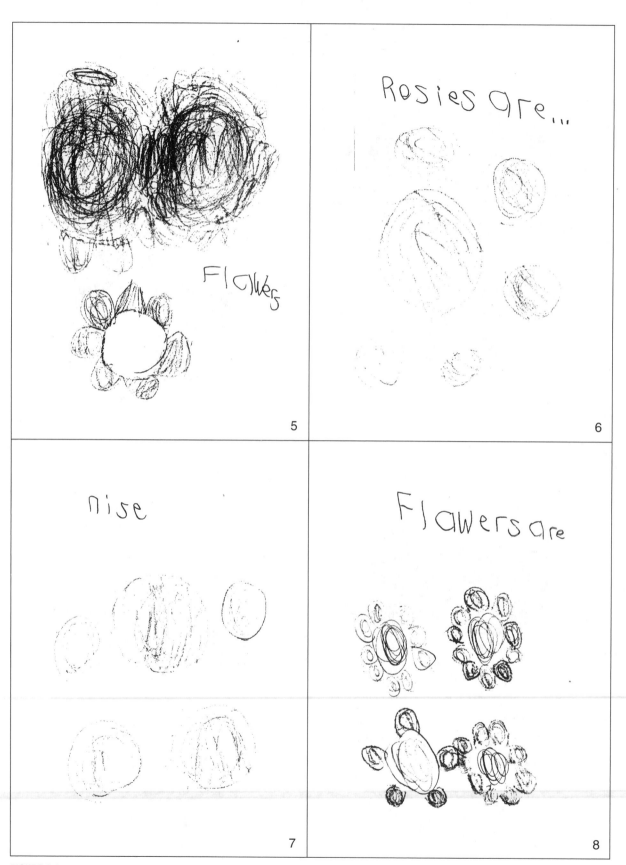

FIGURE 8.1 *continued* (5) Flowers (6) Roses are. . . (7) nice (8) Flowers are.

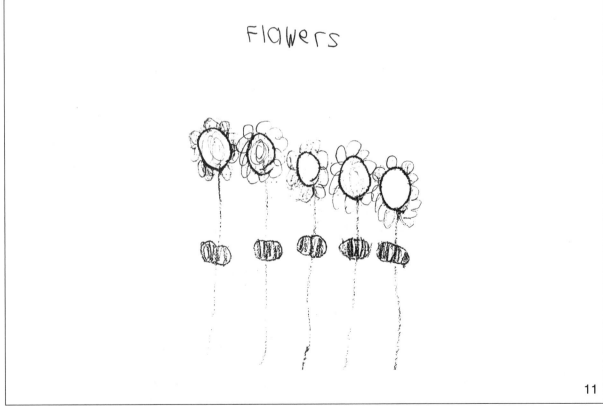

FIGURE 8.1 *continued* (9) nice (10) Daisies are nice so as [are] (11) Flowers.

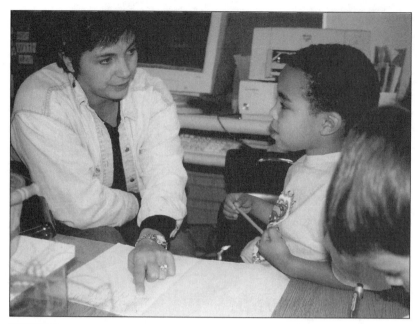

FIGURE 8.2 Angie, Lisa's teaching assistant, and Cedric have a conference.

In our record for Marissa's conference that day, we noted that we talked with her about writing with more fullness on future pieces of writing, and that we gave her a strategy for getting more ideas around a topic. The flower book was no better because of our conference, but Marissa had a better understanding that it was possible for her to write bigger the next time she set out to write about something she knows a lot about.

Typical Kinds of Conferences

So with that mantra guiding us—What might we teach that will help this *writer?*—we engage in continuous assessment (as described in the last chapter) to help us make decisions about what we'll teach in our conferences day after day. Our goal is that our conferences will leave children with energy for the work they're doing and that the teaching will also be leading children toward independence. We try to remember that we are helping children with things today that we want them to be able to do on their own in the future, so we have to frame all our teaching with an eye toward that future independence. We must make sure that at the end of every conference, we leave children with a clear vision for how they might use what we've taught them after we're gone.

Let's think now about some typical kinds of writing conferences we have with our youngest writers.

Helping Children Grab Hold of Ideas and Grow Them

One very simple kind of conference that is fairly common, especially early in the year, is one in which we help children use talk to grab hold of an idea and make it bigger. We want the children to learn that a good writing idea is one they have a lot to say about. Someday, when they are able to write more fluently, they'll learn to use writing to capture their thinking and make their ideas bigger before they draft them. But at this point in their development, we teach them to use talk to do this writing work.

In a conference like this, we simply ask the child to tell us about what he's writing about—his dog, baseball, piano lessons, whatever. Often, we're not even looking at what he's got in the piece of writing at that point. We're talking off it instead. We'll ask questions and make connections to what the child is saying as we try to help him feel the fullness of what he knows about his idea.

When we have generated a good bit of talk about the topic, we help the child think about how he might put some of those ideas into what he's writing. Often we'll flip through different pages and help him envision putting this detail here and that one there. We have to end these conferences by naming for the child what we have done together; this is the teaching part. We have to say something like, "See how we took all those things you know about your little sister and we talked about them and thought about using them in your book? You need to keep doing this when you write new books—talk and think about all you know about your topic that might go in your book. Make sure the idea for your book is big in your head before you start writing about it."

Every now and then we happen upon a child who has clearly chosen a topic that she doesn't have much to say about. This sometimes happens when a child chooses a topic because another writer has chosen it or when a child chooses a topic just because it's safe and she can spell most of the words related to it. When we realize this is the case, we sometimes try to redirect the child toward an idea she really owns with more solid thinking. If we do this, we try to help her understand why it makes sense to do this, again trying to teach her that she needs to choose writing ideas that are full in her thinking.

Helping Children Get Words Down on the Page

Early in the year we have lots of conferences that simply help children get words down on the page, especially children who haven't had much experience with this. This is just one of the biggest deals for our youngest writers and we really have to help them get up and going with this. We also have these conferences when it is clear to us that a child is avoiding challenging words for fear of spelling.

In these conferences we generally will observe the child for a few moments first so we can see what strategies, if any (sometimes we have to start from scratch), she is using to help her generate spellings. We are looking to see if there are any strategies she's not using that we need to help her use, and based on what she's writing, we'll help her use strategies that make sense for the words she's trying to spell.

The strategies we're looking for are

- stretching the word out and saying it slowly to listen to the sounds

- thinking about what a word looks like (if it is one the child has likely seen before)

- thinking about whether the word is a long or short word

- using knowledge of other words and spelling patterns

- using resources in the room

In these conferences we are also helping children remember to put spaces between their words and to reread often so they won't forget what they have written.

FIGURE 8.3 Lisa conferring during writing workshop.

Our goal in these conferences is twofold. First, we want to help children become more independent in their ability to get the words down on the page. Second, we want to help them generate better and better spellings for the words they're using. Because of these goals, we must be sure we point out to them often how it is we are helping them and how they can do this on their own when we're not there. We say things like, "See how you used Hunter's name to help you spell *hunt*? If one word is a part of another word you know, you can spell them the same way."

Sometimes in these conferences we will show children a tricky spelling pattern if it's part of a word they are trying to generate. We don't do this until we have gotten the child over the hump of being willing to try spelling words independently. In other words, if we know the child will try to spell the word without our help, then we might consider helping if we see an opportunity to teach the child an important spelling understanding. Katie watched Helena set out to write the word *nature* once and after writing an *n* and an *a*, Helena stopped, obviously perplexed. "I think this is a tricky word," she said. She likely had a visual picture of the word that contradicted the *ch* sound she heard when she sounded it out. Katie used this as an opportunity to show Helena this spelling and talk about why it was spelled that way.

Helping Children with the Process of Writing

Sometimes we have conferences with children that help them with some aspect of the process of writing. Usually when we have conferences like this it's because we have caught the child in the act of process and we see a logical thing to teach. We pull from our understandings about how children this age use the process (outlined in Chapter 4) as we think about what makes sense for their work.

Sometimes in these conferences we help children think ahead about what they're writing. We'll ask them to tell us about their plans for something they've just started and then we'll name this thinking we're doing as *prewriting*. Sometimes we come across children who seem to be stuck and we may offer suggestions for getting their thinking going again—talking to another child, rereading to get the meaning going again, doing some research to get more ideas, and so on. Sometimes we come across children who aren't using a very good process for composition. Their ideas don't connect well from page to page, or their illustrations really don't enhance the meaning of their words. In these cases we try to help the children refine how they are going about thinking of what comes next in the words or thinking about what should be in their illustrations.

We also look for opportunities to teach children beginning understandings about revising and editing in these conferences, and we find them easily. Revision possibilities come most often in the talk children do around their writing. An amazing thing they tell us that's not on their page becomes a chance to add an important detail. Or a child reads a line, such as "My dog has white spots," and then says, "Well, they're not really white, they're kind of brown," and we have a great opportunity to show him how to strike out *white* and change it to *brown*. We might also read through something and realize a certain part would be better at the end of the book. We show the child how to take the staples out and move the page to the end. We can teach these kinds of revision moves either in the words or the illustrations, but either way we must be sure the child understands why the revision suggestion we're offering makes sense.

The possibilities for editing come about when children are reading their writing to us and it is clear in their reading that they sense something is not down on the page the way it should be. It may be a word that's been left out, a punctuation mark that's missing, or an inflected ending to a spelling that's not there. When we hear that they sense this, we help them figure out how to edit it. We also teach them useful strategies, such as moving their fingers under each word as they read to make sure they're all there or using sticky notes to change a spelling.

Helping Children Imagine New Crafting Possibilities

In these conferences we are looking at what children are doing in their books and then helping them see how various crafting techniques might make their writing better. What matters most in these conferences is that we explain why the technique makes sense in the child's writing and how it will make the writing better. Without this explanation, the writing may get better, but the writer won't have learned anything she might be able to use again on another piece of writing in the future.

Sometimes children are already trying to use some crafting technique on their own and just need a little help. We came upon Ashley one morning and she explained that she wanted to use some "big and bold" words in her book like we had seen Donald Crews use in his books. When we asked her how she thought she'd go about doing this, Ashley said she wasn't sure. The book she was writing was about different kinds of fish, so we suggested she might make the names of the big fish like the sharks and the whales big and bold. With this suggestion we named why it made sense to use the technique with those words—because the print would match the meaning, in this sense of bigness, for the words—and this was the teaching part of the conference.

Sometimes we see what a child is working on and we think of a technique that makes perfect sense in the writing and we suggest it to the child. Often these are techniques we've studied as a class at some point, but not always. For example, one morning as we worked with Michael in a conference and he showed us his dinosaur book, we had an idea for something. He had written on one page, "Raptors can call for help. They're smart." We had been talking about how writers make their writing sound good and one of the ways we'd seen them do this is to use repetition to stretch out an idea. On Michael's raptors page we saw an opportunity for him to try doing this. We suggested he write it like this: "Raptors can call for help. They're smart. *Very smart.*" He liked the suggestion and added that repetitive phrase. We were careful to explain why it made sense for him to do that—it sounded good and it made the idea bigger—and suggested he could do it again if he came to a place where he thought it would work. We even suggested a strategy for him to try repeating things aloud to see how they sounded before he decided whether he wanted to do it in his writing.

We have become quite comfortable with suggesting crafting techniques to children, both for text and for illustrations. We believe this is one way they learn to use techniques to help them write well. We are careful always to base our suggestions in what the child is already writing and to explain why the technique makes sense for the writer so he can try it again at some point on his own in another situation like this.

Helping Children with the Conventions of Writing

Sometimes in conferences we are helping children with the conventions of written language. Most children will need some help with end punctuation at one point or another during the year to help them get control of this most basic use of punctuation. We teach the children to read their writing aloud and to listen for where the end marks go. They can almost always hear where they go because it's difficult to run two sentences together without a voice drop. When we are there with them as they are actually generating sentences, we show them how they can tell when they are at the end of one thing they want to say and need to put a mark before moving on to the next thing.

As for other marks of punctuation, we really just look for opportunities where it makes sense to show children how to use them. When we sit down next to Cassie, who's writing a book called *Mommy's Day* in which a series of different animals are saying "Happy Mommy's Day" to their respective mothers, well, it just makes sense to help her use quotation marks throughout the book. Children will begin using marks such as commas, apostrophes, quotation marks, colons, and ellipses because we've called their attention to them in our minilessons and writing work throughout the day. Sometimes our conferences help them refine what they are already trying to do with punctuation.

Some of the children will need some help with various letter formations or handwriting issues, and if we see this, we will help them with this during writing conferences. If a child is struggling a lot with keeping his writing moving in straight lines but doesn't want to use lined paper, we might make him an "undersheet" of paper with dark, bold lines that he can place under another blank page to help him stay straight.

Late in the year as fluency develops, some students will begin writing the inevitable chapter books and when they do, it's time to show them the convention of paragraph breaks. "When it gets long, break it into a new paragraph," we tell them. This is a very beginning but worthwhile understanding of how paragraphs work to break up longer texts.

Setting Specific Agendas for Individual Children

Sometimes in our conferences we find ourselves setting specific agendas for individual children that help them get over some hump in their writing. Lisa bans all hearts, rainbows, and flowers from Meagan's illustrations until further notice because that's all she ever draws, regardless of what the book is about. Katie tells Cauley he must say at least three things on every page (and she sits there through several pages to be sure he does) because she knows he simply isn't stretching himself enough with the writing part. Lisa makes a rule for Helena that she must write first and then illustrate because she knows she's ready to learn to use the writing to help her think. Jared and Colten are told they must write a few books on their own before they coauthor again because they're becoming too dependent on each other. Sierra is told she may not start another book until she finishes several of the many unfinished ones in her work folder.

Fairly assertive teaching, huh? But we talk very honestly with the children in these conferences about why we need to give them these guidelines for a while in their work. Most of the time our reasoning seems to make sense to them, and we check in with them from time to time to make sure they are following whatever agenda we've set for them.

Giving Children Access to Writer's Language

Writing conferences are the perfect place to really initiate children into using the language of writers and writing. As we watch them write and we listen when they explain to us what they're working on, we use specialized language to say back to them what we see them doing. Take Tayler, for example. When we sat down with her for a writing conference during our poetry genre study, she explained that she was working on a poem about wildcats. The topic of wildcats was one she had lingered with during our earlier study of literary nonfiction. "You're writing about the same topic in a different genre now, aren't you? How smart." We wanted the word *genre* to be a clear part of our teaching in the conference because we realized Tayler's work had set her up to really understand what this word means for her as a writer.

Taking Chances: Trial-and-Error Conferences

Much of the teaching we do in writing conferences feels fairly comfortable for us because we have the confidence of experience behind us. In other words, we've seen what we're suggesting to a particular child be helpful for lots of children in the past. But every now and then we are faced with a real dilemma about the best way to help certain children. When this is the case, our individual work with them becomes a process of trial and error as we try to figure out what kind of help to offer.

At one point during the school year, Katie was trying to decide on the best way to help one child get over the hump of not being able to read back what she'd written. There seemed to be a disconnect between what Josie could read on her own and what she was writing with almost purely phonetic spellings. After trying several different ways of working, Katie decided one day to sit alongside Josie and try a new strategy. As Josie would write each word, Katie asked her to say the word aloud and she (Katie) recorded it on a sticky note. At the end of each page of writing, Katie asked Josie to read the words, not from her page, but from the sticky note they'd attached to the back with Katie's transcription on it. Josie was able to read them.

They worked through four or five pages of the book that way, and even though there was a lot of repetition of words from page to page, Josie never looked at Katie's writing on the sticky notes that were stuck to the backs of previous pages. She generated the text anew each time, saying the words aloud as she wrote them, and then read what she'd written from Katie's transcription. But by the end of that day's workshop, Josie and Katie realized that they could both read what Josie was writing from her original page; they didn't need the sticky note transcriptions anymore. The extended interaction seemed to help Josie realize that when she puts words down on the page, they need to look more like words she has seen in her reading.

As we teachers talked about our conferences that day, Katie explained what she had tried and that it was something she had never done before. She explained she was hesitant to try it because she felt transcribing a child's writing can send a negative message, and because she was afraid Josie might decide she couldn't do it on her own and would just want to copy the transcribed words. Neither of these fears was realized, however, and that day of trial and error seemed to pay off in a big way for Josie in her writing. When we tried the same strategy a few days later with another writer, it didn't help him at all. He *did* decide he couldn't do it on his own, and we spent several days undoing the setback of a strategy that didn't help.

We tell this story not because we think the strategy is one that should necessarily be replicated, but simply to make the point that sometimes in our conferences we just have to try something and see if it helps a child. Again, though, we have to remember as we do this that our goal is for the child to become more independent from the work we do alongside her.

Without a doubt, conferencing with children on a regular basis is a very necessary part of helping them really develop as writers in the context of a writing workshop. We get them up and writing, and then we go out and teach, teach, teach alongside them.

Share Time as Another Time for Teaching

One aspect of working with our youngest writers that is quite different from our work with older writers is the extent to which they are sharing

FIGURE 8.4 Whitley and Michael share as they are writing.

writing as they are producing it. The movement between thinking, talk-ing, and writing is almost seamless for young writers, and so anyone sitting anywhere near another writer during workshop is almost certainly privy to what everyone around him is writing. If they need response, they very naturally say, "Hey, Joshua, listen to this. . . ." Our writing workshops with young writers stay noisy with sharing, so in this sense, we don't feel as much of a need for sanctioned response groups that meet on a regular basis as we often do with older writers.

Still, each day's workshop ends with a time for sharing from our writing work. This time usually lasts about ten minutes and we think of it as another time for teaching. As we are conferencing each day, we're on the lookout for smart work we see children doing. When we find smart work, we ask those children to share their writing for very specific reasons—they've done something in the actual text or in the process of writing it that we want other children to know about. Usually, the child reads the writing and then Lisa talks around it to help the other children notice what it is she wants them to see.

In addition to the day-to-day sharing of smart work, here are some other ways we have children share their writing with others:

- We may simply ask children to share writing in twos and threes before they put it back in their folders at the end of writing workshop.

- We encourage children to have peer conferences at any time during writing workshop if they need help or need to get some response.

- At the end of a unit of study, we may have a more extended period of sharing from what we've learned in the study.

- Children may visit other classrooms to share their writing. These don't have to be other young classes; they may be fourth- or fifth-grade classes.

- Children may sign up for an appointment with the principal to share a favorite piece of writing.

- We may invite parents in once or twice a year for a celebration of shared writing.

The Kinds of Things Writers Make and How We'll Make Them in This Room

This series of lessons makes sense as a beginning-of-the-year study for students who have never been in a writing workshop, which is most of our students in first grade. We have set them up with the idea that they are to "make stuff" during writing workshop each day, and this study is meant to show them the kinds of things they might make and to help them understand the structures that are in place to help them make those things in this room. The goal of this series of lessons is really quite simple: we want it to launch everyone into independent bookmaking. We are not going to worry about the quality of what they're making at this point; that's for our later teaching. This study is just to get them started making stuff.

Over the course of this study, we will look at a variety of examples of published writing that children in previous writing workshops have done. In almost any study we plan, we try to think of ways to have students look at what first-grade writers in years past have done. We find that these lessons are particularly meaningful because the writers who produced these books really are just like them—in age and size and experience—many of them ride the same bus or attend the same church, and sometimes they are even siblings.

UNIT OF STUDY A
The Kinds of Things Writers Make and
How We'll Make Them in This Room

As we share this writing, we'll try to have a good range of ability levels represented so the children will think, "I could do something like that." We will walk through these books and point out things we want the children to notice, both in the illustrations and in the words. We'll also share the inside story of how the pieces of writing came to be—things like "Aaron went fishing with his dad, and that's where he got the idea for this," or "Diane Seibert was Anna's favorite writer, and that's why she decided to write it in first person this way."

Our goal is to show children a range of kinds of writing they might do, so we'll be sure to look at different genres, but we'll also likely look at other writing ideas as well—writing that's been done for specific audiences, writing that's been coauthored, writing that has photographs incorporated in it, writing where a child was creating a series, and so forth. We make sure that these minilessons always end with us envisioning what it would be like if someone in the room *this year* tried some writing like this. Our goal for these lessons is for children to have lots of ideas for kinds of things they'd like to make.

During this study, we might also begin to turn children's attention to the writing of professionals. Often we do this by putting professional writing alongside the children's writing—Frog and Toad books alongside Maggie and Larke's series (Chapter 1), for example. When we do this we make sure the children understand that Maggie and Larke were doing the same kind of writing thing as Arnold Lobel. Or we might just show the children something a professional writer has done with writing that they might try—writing a concept book like Tana Hoban or writing a book that's a conversation like *Yo! Yes?* by Chris Raschka. See the chart in the "Resources for Getting Started" section (page 158) for other kinds of things we might show children that they could try with writing.

When this study happens at the beginning of the year, we are likely to layer in some teaching about how children are to get this kind of writing work accomplished. We'll deal with any management issues we see happening in the room, but in addition to that, we'll address two topics we know will be issues: spelling and finishing. We'll take a few days of minilessons just to teach children the strategies we want them to use when they are unsure about the spelling of a word (detailed in Chapter 4). As a part of these strategy lessons, we might show students examples of tough words children have tackled in the past. We'll also take a few minilessons to explain our expectations for finishing (detailed in Chapter 2), and again, we are likely to use student examples to help them see what these expectations look like when they are fulfilled in a piece of writing.

FIGURE A.1 A typical beginning book written during this study. There's lots of teaching work still to do, but this author is on his way! Notice the print inside the illustrations—something he's seen other writers do in their books. (1) The sinking boat book. (2) The sinking boat. (3) One time me and Dad saw a sunken boat. (4) We read a pirate book.

FIGURE A.1 *continued* (5) Pirates are mean.

Resources for Getting Started

> ### OTHER KINDS OF THINGS TO TRY WHEN MAKING BOOKS
>
> • a book with illustrations only and no words
> • a book that labels the pictures
> • a book with some photographs in it
> • an alphabet book
> • a book with some singing or music in it
> • a book organized by colors
> • a book with pictures that pop up
> • a book with different poems in it
> • a book with some facts in it
> • a counting book
> • a lift-the-flap book
> • a question–and–answer book

Where Writers Get Ideas

Since students are going to be expected to write every single day, all year long, one issue they will inevitably face is that of topic selection. Now, they won't need a new topic every day. They'll work on many of their books for a number of days at a time, and many of them will use the same topic again and again to do different kinds of writing. But topic selection over time is an issue, and we want them making thoughtful choices about what they are writing about, not just choosing something offhandedly. So a series of minilessons about where and how people who write books get their ideas can be especially helpful early in the year, or later in the year, when energy for topic finding may be waning or children may not be making thoughtful choices.

In a study of where writers get their ideas and how they choose topics to pursue, we'll try to stay focused on a few simple, big ideas. Basically, we want children to know that writers often write about things they know a lot about, things that are very familiar; writers often write about the same topics again and again, in different ways, in different books; and writers often get ideas for writing when they are away from their desks, when they're not writing. Writers notice, listen, observe, and think like writers all the time.

To help us get our thinking going in this study, we might return to some of the writing we've already looked at that children have done in the past (or look at new examples) and talk very specifically about where and how the children got the ideas for these pieces of writing.

A good number of our lessons in this study will probably come from reading book flaps, authors' notes, and dedications in books that give information about how writers have chosen topics. We might read excerpts from interviews with writers students know or watch videos of authors talking about where they get ideas and how they do their writing. We can also simply revisit any book we've read and talk about where we *think* the writer may have gotten the idea. It's not so important that we are right when we have a conversation like this. Our goal is to get students thinking about the fact that, before there can be a book, there has to be a writer who has an idea.

Whenever we discuss how a writing idea came to be, it is critical that we dig out the "what there is to know about writing" from what is said. For example, if we show the students Michael's book from last year about dinosaurs and tell them he chose this topic because he had lots of books about dinosaurs at home, we name this in a general way as "Sometimes writers write about things they have studied and know a lot about." We then help the children envision finding a writing idea in this same way.

When looking at books and thinking about the ideas behind them, at some point it seems useful to look at a stack of different books by the same author. We might stack up our Nicola Davies books and determine that she writes a lot about animals, or put all our Donald Crews books together and see that he often writes about things that move—trucks, boats, trains, parades, and so on. As we do this, we try to remember we are teaching students who, at the end of the year, will have a whole collection of books they have written about topics they have chosen. Looking at how a single author has made many topic decisions over time really helps students imagine the kind of writing lives *they* could have over time. And of course, the collections of writing students will create are so important to the sense of self they'll develop as writers—Forrest writes a lot about animals, Megan is good at books about friends, Levi has very intricate illustrations. . . . As a part of this line of thinking, we might show students a few series of books, too—Henry and Mudge, the Arthur books, Frog and Toad—and talk to them about this kind of writing so that they might consider it as a possibility for their own work.

We might use a survey of the room during this study and look at the kinds of things the children are writing about and then discuss how they are deciding on these topics. We could chart this by asking the children what topics they are currently writing about. Or we might have just one or two children bring their folders to the minilesson and, using a fishbowl format, go through the folders and talk about how they got their ideas for each piece. This would demonstrate how to think and talk about where we get ideas, something we'd expect everyone to be thinking and talking about during the course of the study.

FIGURE B.1 Sometimes an idea comes because we want to do some writing for a specific audience—as Cassey did for her mom when Cassey's grandmother passed away. A quite sophisticated choice for her to make as a beginning writer. (1) My Mamaw. (2) My mamaw is in heaven. (3) She is an angel. (4) She loves to fly.

FIGURE B.1 *continued* (5) You can't see her. (6) My mawmaw (is) nice because she loves me. (7) My mawmaw is in a better place.

And finally, if we do any writing ourselves, we can teach some lessons in this study from our own experiences. When we do this, we show students pieces of writing we have done and explain to them how we chose the topic of the writing.

After this study, "Where did you get the idea for this?" will become a standard assessment question for all the children's writing. This part of the process, the part where a writer thinks about what she should write about, has been made visible by the study and now will be something we'll continue to talk about. We'll expect students to use the language of the study to be more articulate about why they have chosen to write about the things they write about.

Resources for Getting Started

The following chart lists books appropriate for our youngest writers in which authors' voices tell us something about the origins of the ideas for the books. A fair number of the voices are found in quotes on the paper book jackets of hardcover editions; the others can be found in authors' notes and dedications inside the books themselves. The books are grouped by the different understandings we can get from what they say about the origin of the ideas. We can all think of lots of other books that likely came from these same idea places, though we may not have the authors' voices to tell us that directly. The key, of course, is to share these understandings and then help children envision getting ideas for their writing in these same ways.

AN IDEA CAN COME FROM THINGS THAT HAPPEN OFTEN IN OUR EVERYDAY LIVES.

So Much. 1994. Trish Cooke, illus. by Helen Oxenbury.

Mud. 1996. Mary Lyn Ray, illus. by Lauren Stringer.

Big Truck, Little Truck. 2000. Jan Carr, illus. by Ivan Bates.

AN IDEA CAN COME FROM A PLACE WE NEVER WANT TO FORGET.

Knoxville, Tennessee. 1994. Nikki Giovanni, illus. by Larry Johnson.

What You Know First. 1995. Patricia MacLachlan, illus. by Barry Moser.

AN IDEA CAN COME FROM A SPECIFIC EXPERIENCE.

"Let's Get a Pup!" Said Kate. 2001. Bob Graham.

Tulip Sees America. 1998. Cynthia Rylant, illus. by Lisa Desimini.

The Barn Owls. 2000. Tony Johnston, illus. by Deborah Kogan Ray.

AN IDEA CAN COME FROM SOMETHING WE WANT OTHER PEOPLE TO UNDERSTAND THE SAME WAY WE UNDERSTAND IT.

A Cool Drink of Water. 2002. Barbara Kerley.

Crab Moon. 2000. Ruth Horowitz, illus. by Kate Kiesler.

Walk with a Wolf. 1997. Janni Howker, illus. by Sarah Fox-Davies.

AN IDEA CAN COME FROM A PLACE WE KNOW WELL.

Out of the Ocean. 1998. Debra Frazier.

Raven and River. 1997. Nancy White Carlstrom, illus. by Jon Van Zyle.

AN IDEA CAN COME FROM SOMETHING WE LOVE TO DO.

Meeting Trees (1997) and *Crawdad Creek* (1999). Scott Russell Sanders, illus. by Robert Hynes.

Stranger in the Woods. 2000. Carl R. Sams II and Jean Stoick.

AN IDEA CAN COME FROM MEMORIES ABOUT A TIME IN OUR LIVES WE CHERISH.

Fishing in the Air. 2000. Sharon Creech, illus. by Chris Raschka.

Mice and Beans. 2001. Pam Muñoz Ryan, illus. by Joe Cepeda.

Meeting Trees (1997) and *Crawdad Creek* (1999). Scott Russell Sanders, illus. by Robert Hynes.

AN IDEA CAN COME FROM A MEMORY OF A SPECIFIC EVENT WE DON'T WANT TO FORGET.

The Christmas Gift / El regalo de Navidad. 2000. Francisco Jiménez, illus. by Claire B. Cotts.

Flying over Brooklyn. 1999. Myron Uhlberg, illus. by Gerald Fitzgerald.

AN IDEA CAN COME FROM PEOPLE WE NEVER WANT TO FORGET.

Quinnie Blue. 2000. Dinah Johnson, illus. by James Ransome.

The Trip Back Home. 2000. Janet S. Wong, illus. by Bo Jia.

Two Mrs. Gibsons. 1996. Toyomi Igus, illus. by Daryl Wells.

AN IDEA CAN COME FROM SOME CHANGE IN OUR LIVES THAT MAKES US THINK AND WONDER.

Castles, Caves, and Honeycombs. 2001. Linda Ashman, illus. by Lauren Stringer.

I Loved You Even Before You Were Born. 2001. Anne Bowen, illus. by Greg Shed.

How to Read
Like Writers

All of our product studies during the year that have anything to do with the techniques of writing will stand on the shoulders of this study. Our goal in this series of lessons is to teach students to read like writers, to notice *how things are written* (the craft of the writing) and then to envision possibilities for their own writing from what they notice. We want the study to give them some beginning language to comment on what they notice—language like *structure, word choice, approach*—as we know they won't have heard people talking about writing in these ways before. We don't have any specific craft techniques in mind for this study that we want students to know in the end; our only goal is that they learn to read like writers.

For this study, we'll look at lots of published writing (in a variety of genres) that we have selected because we know it is full of things for the children to notice about how it is written. We'll look for interesting uses of language, punctuation, text structure, print, and illustrations, introducing all the features of texts we're likely to study in more depth in later studies. Many of the books we'll study will be written by professional authors, but some of them may be books written by former students.

During this study we will also begin to really emphasize the way writing *sounds* when we read it. We want the children to begin to hear the way things are written. We know that over time they'll come to understand how different crafting techniques make writing sound a certain way. Very often when we're reading aloud, we will stop and reread something that has a particularly nice sound to it, asking the

FIGURE C.1 In this excerpt from *Rainforest Adventures,* Autumn shows us she knows how to invite her reader to participate in the text by addressing the reader directly as *you*. Lisa and the children call this crafting technique the "tour guide" effect. (1) The Rainforest Adventures. Enter here. (2) When you go inside Rainforest Adventures you will see a gift shop and then, you will see a tunnel and inside that tunnel you will see reptiles (snake, turtle, alligator).

children to focus on really listening to it. We also want them to have the sound of good writing echoing inside them as they write so they'll know when writing sounds *right*.

We have found it helpful in the early lessons in this study just to show children some things in books to help them develop writers' eyes. For several days we either revisit books we've read during the year for other reasons or we look at new books, and we point out crafting techniques the writers are using in the books. For example, we might take Jane and Christopher Kurtz's *Water Hole Waiting* (2002) and show the children how they write it in present tense like it's happening as you read it. We'd read through some of the noun–verb phrases so they could hear them happening now—"morning slinks . . . crickets stop . . . a frog plops." We might show them the giraffe page and talk with them about the variety of craft techniques we see on that one page:

> *Gulup, galumpf.* Giraffe is swaying down the path. Time mooooves slow . . . o . . . owly around Giraffe. Neck bends, legs splay. Will lips ever go so low that they touch the water?

TECHNIQUES

- making up a word to match a sound (onomatopoeia)
- manipulating print and spelling to match the meaning
- using ellipses to show passing of time
- two short, subject–verb sentences combined to show one continuous action
- using a question to engage the reader

And we might end by showing them how the structure of the book follows a course from morning to evening and how the authors include an authors' note in the end that explains some of what happens in the book. Often, these conversations become layered as the children think of other books they know where a writer is doing something similar to what we are showing them. We always end these lessons with envisioning what it would look like if someone in the room tried some of these techniques in his or her writing.

After several days of showing them things, we will begin to use walk-throughs and small-group inquiry (Chapter 5) to let the children tell us what they notice about how things are written. We always love this part of the study because the children so often notice things that we didn't see when we looked at a book, and because this is where they begin to see that lots of writers use the same kinds of techniques in lots of different kinds of books. We chart their noticings and talk about them

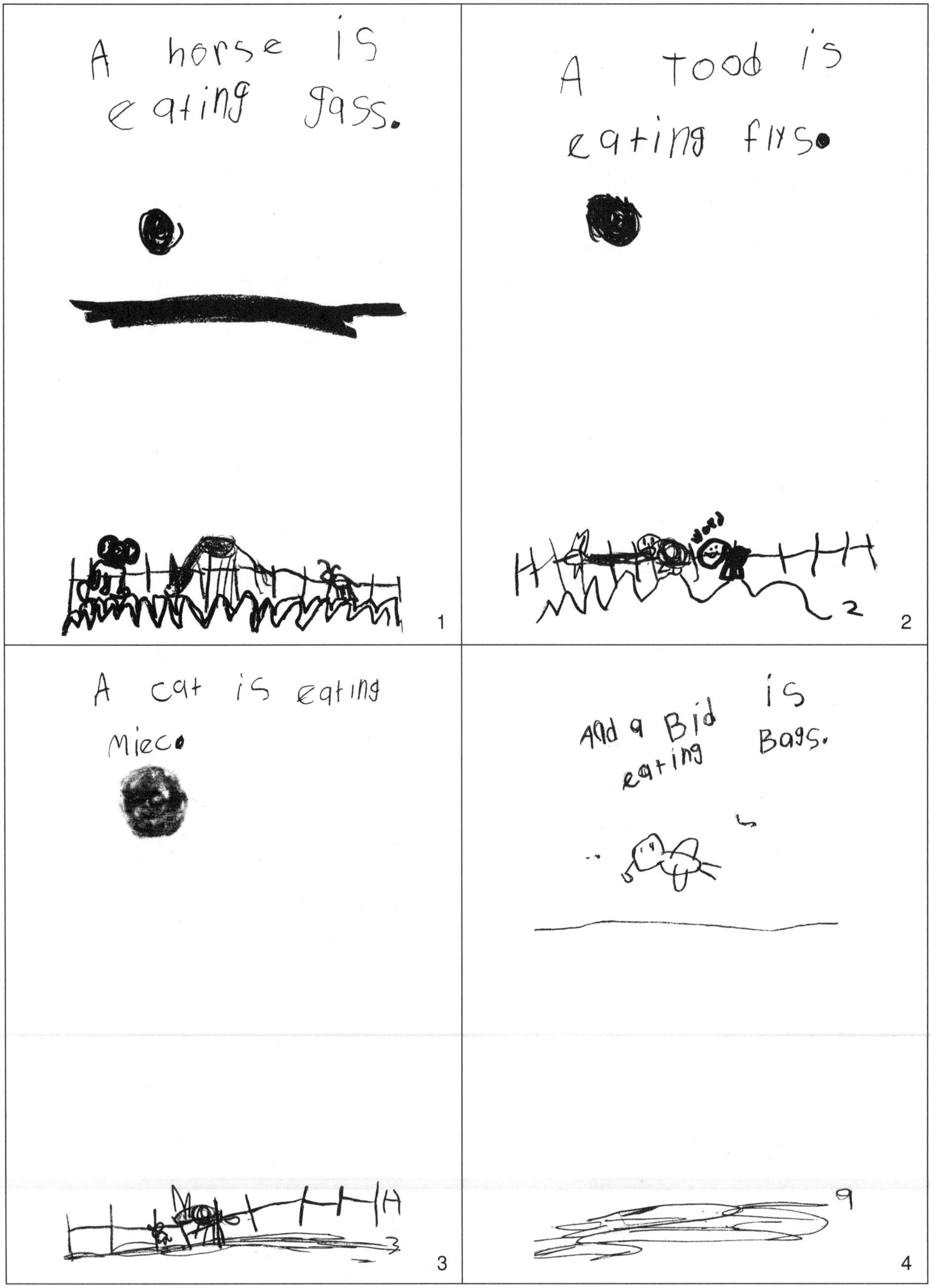

FIGURE C.2 In this excerpt from *Animal Food and Animals*, Michaela shows us she knows exactly how to use *and* to start the last sentence in a series of sentences (there are nine sentences in all in the whole book)—a kind of ending she's seen in lots of books that are structured in this way. (1) A horse is eating grass. (2) A toad is eating flies. (3) A cat is eating mice. (4) And a bird is eating bugs.

until we can envision someone in the room trying the techniques they've seen used by professional writers.

After this study we expect to see two main things happening. First, we expect children to continue to read like writers as we encounter new books along the way. We'll find time whenever we can to ask, "What did you notice about how this was written?" Second, we expect to see children trying out some of the crafting techniques we have talked about and envisioned during the study. We may even require them to have one piece that represents their best attempts to use what they've learned from the study. And for sure, "What decisions did you make about craft in this piece of writing?" will become a standard assessment question in the room after this study. Over time, if we keep asking, children will know we expect them to be able to answer that question about their writing.

Resources for Getting Started

The following chart lists ten books appropriate for young writers that are good starter books in a study of how to read like writers because they have crafting techniques that the children notice easily. With each book we've noted a few of the main text features we'll likely talk about when we share the books with the children in this study. Remember that many of these techniques are ones we'll study more deeply in later, more focused studies.

The real value of a list like this is not the specific books it names, for hundreds of other books would serve just as well. The value is in seeing the *kinds* of books we might select and for what reasons.

EARTHDANCE. 1996. JOANNE RYDER, ILLUS. BY NORMAN GORBATY.

- written with a second-person "you," engaging the reader directly in the text
- lots of interesting positioning of the print on the page in meaningful ways
- rich use of language, especially strong verbs *(streaked with roads and bridges)*
- personification of an inanimate object

GRANDPA NEVER LIES. 2000. RALPH FLETCHER, ILLUS. BY HARVEY STEVENSON.

- strong text structure—moves clearly through the seasons
- strong text structure—a line that is repeated at the end of each vignette *(And Grandpa never lies, so I know it's true)* and then a twist on the repeated line at the very end of the book

- details from the beginning of the story are mentioned again in the end

- rich use of language *(diamonds dance)* and lots of complex sentences stretched out and slowed down with commas

THE GREAT GRACIE CHASE. 2001. CYNTHIA RYLANT, ILLUS. BY MARK TEAGUE.

- repetition used in the same way across a series of sentences

- all sorts of interesting punctuation usage—parentheses, exclamation marks, commas

- environmental print incorporated into illustrations

- lots of print manipulations with capital letters and italics for emphasis

IN MY NEW YELLOW SHIRT. 2001. EILEEN SPINELLI, ILLUS. BY HIDEKO TAKAHASHI.

- strong text structure—repeated phrase used to tie vignettes together

- all sorts of punctuation used—ellipses, dashes, quotation marks

- rich language use *(daffodil dancing dizzily)*

- repetition of the same detail (Sam's face) across lots of illustrations

LOKI AND ALEX: THE ADVENTURES OF A DOG AND HIS BEST FRIEND. 2001. CHARLES R. SMITH.

- A text can move back and forth between two characters who are narrating the same events.

- Illustrations can be rendered so readers see things the way a particular narrator would see them.

- A text can be written (in its entirety) as people talking.

- A text can have an author's note in the beginning that explains something about how it is written.

MOTHERS ARE LIKE THAT. 2000. CAROL CARRICK, ILLUS. BY PAUL CARRICK.

- use of a repeated line throughout a very simple text

- sentences stretched out over several pages with little details added each time

- illustrations show lots of variations of the more general topic of the book: mothers

- illustrations show a twist at the end

Mud. 1996. Mary Lyn Ray, illus. by Lauren Stringer.

- lead fashioned to make us wonder—a pronoun *(it)* with no antecedent
- rich use of language, especially lots of attention to sound in word choice *(run rattling in the flapping wind)*
- series of short, two-word sentences with very strong verbs
- some interesting interactions between words and illustrations

Nocturne. 1997. Jane Yolen, illus. by Anne Hunter.

- simple structure of a repeated phrase connecting vignettes
- several examples of internal repetition of words
- rich use of language—adjectives used to stretch out the noun night in each repeated phrase, surprising word choices (*deep* feathers, *silent* passages), and so on
- some wordplay with made-up words (q*uiltdown* and *quietdown*)

Psssst! It's Me . . . the Bogeyman. 1998. Barbara Park, illus. by Stephen Kroninger.

- interesting approach to the writing—as if the narrator is speaking directly to the reader
- lots of manipulations of print (size, shape, appearance) for meaning
- all sorts of interesting punctuation usage—dashes, parentheses, ellipses, and so on
- interesting manipulations of spelling to match voice and sound (*w-w-weren't* and *whissssper*).

Rain. 2000. Manya Stojic.

- strong text structure—moving through a series of animals leading up to an event (rainstorm), and then back through them after the event
- lots of print manipulations for meaning—size and bold
- an ending that matches the beginning and uses similar repetition
- lots of illustrations that seem to run off the edges of the pages

Finding Writing Mentors

One thing we believe is important for children to understand is how to apprentice themselves to writers whose work they admire. Most craftspeople tell us they study the work of other master craftspeople—actors and actresses study the films of others they admire, art students copy famous paintings as practice, musicians listen to the same bars played over and over by other master musicians. In this series of lessons, our goal is to help children understand that good writers can be their mentors and show them all kinds of new possibilities for their writing when they get to know those mentors well. As a result of this study, we expect children to begin talking about professional writers by name and to be able to talk about what they know about different writers' work across texts, for example, "Frank Asch usually illustrates with watercolor," or "Mem Fox uses a lot of rhythm in her writing," or "Eric Carle puts some of the same illustrations in different books."

For this study, as we read like writers, we'll be looking at stacks of published texts by single authors (taking several days or even a couple of weeks to study one author), and our minilessons will be a combination of just showing students things in texts, walking through them together and noticing, and doing some small-group inquiry. As much as possible, we'll try to talk *across* the stacks and notice craft techniques the individual writers use often in different pieces of writing. "As we look at all these books, what can we say about this writer's style?" is a question that guides us.

FIGURE D.1 Cele illustrates with watercolors after learning that Frank Asch uses watercolors in his illustrations.

We like to choose two or three authors to study together as a whole class. We may do these in a single long study of finding mentor authors, or we may spread the studies of individual authors out over time and have different studies in between. We try to choose writers whose work we know the children like, and we often look for writers who illustrate their own books because our students both write and illustrate their books. We need to choose writers who have a body of work we can consider, at least four or five books, and we need to choose writers we know craft in some very intentional ways. We also look for writers who have published a variety of kinds of books on a variety of topics.

We have to make sure that at some point after we have studied some mentor authors together and tried writing under the influence of that study (using crafting techniques we've learned from authors in our own writing), we then find ways to nudge children to find mentors on their own. There are several ways we might do this. In Lisa's workshop, after their initial studies of mentor authors, a standard assessment question is, "Did you stand on an author's shoulders to write this? If so, whose?" That's our way of asking if they used some craft technique(s) in the piece that they learned from a mentor author. We might also have a unit in which groups of children choose their own mentor authors to study and then teach others what they have learned from their different mentors. And certainly we can organize books by author from time to time so we make it easy for students to read through a mentor author's work on their own.

Panel 1 (Editing Sheet):

Editing Sheet

Name of Author(s) Tayler

Name of illustrator(s) Tayler

Check your punctuation... yes ✓ . ... ? Yes ✓ !

Can you read your words ? Yes ✓

Do you have all the words that you need ? Yes ✓

Have you checked your spelling ? Yes ✓

Did you use some kind of craft ? Yes ✓ If so, what?
Refrindn

Did you stand on an Authors shoulders? Yes ✓ If so, then
Who? Frank asch

What we worked on: II work on spelling things —
an lo

Panel 2: I What avery Waver

Panel 3: I whet sweming in the sea.

Panel 4: I what woking in the diserd it was vaver hot.

FIGURE D.2 As Tayler states on her editing sheet, Frank Asch was her mentor for *I Went Everywhere*. She uses a repeating line in much the same way that he does in *The Earth and I*. (2) I went everywhere. (3) I went swimming in the sea. (4) I went walking in the desert. It was very hot.

FIGURE D.2 *continued* (5) I went everywhere. (6) I went to an aquarium. It was cold. (7) I went in a deep and cold, cold pool. (8) I went everywhere.

Resources for Getting Started

A VERY SHORT LIST OF A FEW AUTHORS WHO FIT SOME OR ALL OF
OUR MENTOR CRITERIA FOR OUR YOUNGEST WRITERS:

- Frank Asch
- Eric Carle
- Donald Crews
- Lois Ehlert
- Denise Fleming
- Mem Fox
- Rachel Isadora
- Joanne Ryder
- Cynthia Rylant
- Charlotte Zolotow

How to Structure Texts in Interesting Ways

We believe that a strong sense of text structure and the ability to make all the parts of a text work together are absolutely essential to effective writing, so in this study we introduce children to the idea of text structure. We want them to begin to think of the simple texts they write as having parts that should work together, and we want them to begin to be intentional when structuring their own texts. This series of lessons will show them some different options for how to do this work. As with all our studies, our goal is not that students will know any specific set of structure options; our goal is that they will have the tools to think differently (structurally) about the texts they create.

During this study we will look mostly at published writing where a very obvious text structure is at work. We might be studying, for example, how *When the Wind Stops*, by Charlotte Zolotow (1995), moves through a long series of questions and answers. Sometimes we'll tuck a student's example of using a text structure in with a stack of published texts showing that structure at work. We'll do a lot of showing at first, helping the children see how the structures work in the texts, and then as the study grows we'll do more teaching in which we ask the children to notice how a text is structured.

We try always to have at least two examples of a structure at work in two different texts because this helps the children see that the structure is not tied to the topic. "Writing through a series of questions and answers" becomes a much clearer option for children to understand when

FIGURE E.1 Jordan uses the days of the week to help him structure a text about his friend Autumn. (1) Me and Autumn are friends. Written by Jordan. Illustrated by Autumn. (2) On Monday me and Autumn play tag when we go outside. (3) On Tuesday me and Autumn play dogs. (4) On Wednesday me and Autumn play catch.

On Thursday Me and Autumn
Play at water
Hav Frea setrse. Whe he We

On Friday Me and Autumn
Play at Legos.

5

6

FIGURE E.1 *continued* (5) On Thursday me and Autumn play at water when we have free centers. (6) On Friday me and Autumn play at Legos®.

they see that Reeve Lindbergh did this in *What Is the Sun?* (1994) just as Charlotte Zolotow did in *When the Wind Stops.* Sometimes we'll show both examples in the same minilesson; sometimes we'll show them in separate lessons. And with every structural option we consider in the minilessons, we spend time envisioning what it would sound like if someone in the room tried writing about one of his or her favorite topics using this structure. "How could Marissa use this structure—a series of questions and answers—to write about flowers, her favorite topic?"

During and after this study, we expect to see children trying different text structures in their writing. We don't assign the children specific structures to try; we want them to choose them on their own (and we'll probably require them to choose) from the variety of options we've found during the study. We believe that deciding on a text structure is a big part of the thinking a writer has to do. We may decide to require the children to write two pieces about the same topic but use different text structures in them. We also expect that structure will continue to be one of the features we notice and talk about with all the texts we encounter in future studies.

One of the interesting outcomes of this study that we have seen time and again is that many children begin to think of their texts as a

FIGURE E.2 Kayla uses a predictable ending to each vignette as a structural device in her book *Sea Creatures*. (1) Sea Creatures (2) Octopuses live in caves. When they are attacked they spread ink! That's what octopuses do. (3) Sharks have a whole lot of teeth. There is one way to kill a shark. Punch it in the gills. That's what sharks do. (4) Dolphins have a loud voice and you can pet them. And they jump jump jump jump. Dolphins do that.

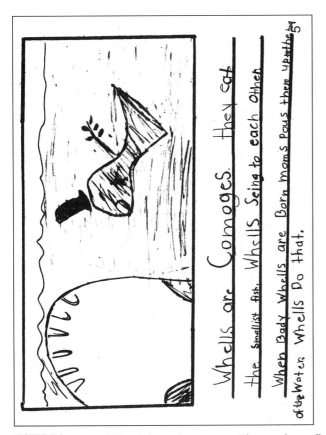

FIGURE E.2 *continued* (5) Whales are humongous. They eat the smallest fish. Whales sing to each other. When baby whales are born moms push them up to the top of the water. Whales do that.

whole in the midst of drafting it. If you catch them in the middle of a draft that has a strong text structure, it's very likely that they can talk you through the parts that aren't even written yet all the way to the ending. In many ways, writing with a strong text structure in mind seems to give them a tangible way to think into the future of their drafts and stretches them past just making it up as they go.

We are long-searching in this work with text structure. The texts the children write are short and very, very simple. The texts themselves may not seem too impressive when they stand alone. But if we look at the writers who created them, we are impressed with the critical under-standing the children gain that a text *should* be structured. We know this understanding will serve them well as they write more and more sophisti-cated texts throughout their writing lives. And of course, many of the options we explore with them and that they use to fashion short, simple texts can be used to structure parts of much longer, more sophisticated texts, so the options are long-searching as well.

Resources for Getting Started

The following list contains ten examples of text structures we have found that help beginning writers understand structure (we wouldn't necessarily look at all of these in a single structure study). We've also included two examples of texts we might use to show each structure to our youngest writers.

- beginnings and endings that match
  The Trip Back Home, Janet S. Wong
  The Relatives Came, Cynthia Rylant

- A repeated phrase that ties vignettes together or is a transitional device
  In My New Yellow Shirt, Eileen Spinelli
  Mothers Are Like That, Carol Carrick

- a series of questions and answers
  Do You Know What I'll Do? Charlotte Zolotow
  Winter Lullaby, Barbara Seuling

- a single question with a series of answers
  Daughter, Have I Told You? Rachel Coyne
  I Want to Be, Thylias Moss

- a text that moves clearly through a time period—a day, a week, months, seasons
  A South African Night, Rachel Isadora
  What a Wonderful Day to Be a Cow, Carolyn Lesser

- a text that moves predictably back and forth between two kinds of content
  Before I Was Your Mother, Kathryn Lasky
  The Two Mrs. Gibsons, Toyomi Igus

- a text structured by the alphabet
  A Mountain Alphabet, Margaret Ruurs
  Into the A, B, Sea, Deborah Lee Rose

- a text that moves through a series of places, people, animals
  So Much, Trish Cooke
  Rain, Manya Stojic

- a text that moves through a *physical* place (takes the reader on a tour)
  Let's Go Home, Cynthia Rylant
  My New York, Kathy Jakobsen

- a text that moves through a series of colors
  All the Colors of the Earth, Sheila Hamanaka
  Chidi Only Likes Blue, Ifeoma Onyefulu

How to Make Illustrations Work Better with Written Text

Our youngest writers will illustrate much of what they write, so we believe it makes sense to study illustrations and how they work to make meaning in conjunction with the written words in a picture book. Our goal in this series of lessons is to nudge children to look very closely at the decisions illustrators are making in the books they read and then to become more decisive, intentional illustrators of their own books. We want the room to be filled with options and possibilities for what children might try in their illustrations, but just as with our other product studies, we don't go into this study planning to cover a specific set of illustration techniques. The techniques we do discover and introduce along the way are simply means to another, more important end: more decisive, intentional illustrators.

In this study, once again, we'll be looking mostly at published picture books and any relevant student work we have from years past. Many of these may be books we have studied for other reasons in other studies, but this time we are going to be looking closely at the illustrations. The progression of the study will be very similar to that of other product studies. We are likely to begin by showing students different things about illustrations in our earliest minilessons. This will get the idea of looking at an illustrator's decisions going in the room and show students the kinds of things we want them to notice. For example, we might return to Cynthia Rylant's book *Scarecrow* (1998), illustrated by

Lauren Stringer, and use it to introduce the idea of studying illustrations to the children. We might point out these kinds of things:

- Illustrations can picture a subject from many different angles throughout the book—sometimes up very close and sometimes far away.

- There can be a story happening in the pictures that isn't happening in the words (the little girl working in the garden throughout the text).

- The passing of time can be shown through the changes that time brings about in the illustrations (we follow the changing seasons in the illustrations).

- Sometimes illustrations cover the entire page spread, sometimes only part of it. Sometimes they are boxed off with white space around them for the words.

- The written words can be placed in a variety of places in relation to the illustrations, and this may vary from page to page.

As we show students these decisions an illustrator has made in a text, we will do the same envisioning we do in all our product studies: we'll think aloud with them about what it would look like if one of them illustrated a book in this way.

As quickly as possible, we'll want to begin letting them tell us what they notice in the illustrations of selected texts. They usually show us they are ready for this fairly quickly. We know they're ready when they begin interrupting our lessons to show us something we never even noticed! At that point, we'll begin to walk through books with them on some days and on other days we'll send them off in twos and threes to study books in small-group inquiry. It's not necessary that they all be studying the same books when we do this. We may use a range of texts from either the same illustrator or a variety of illustrators. When we share what they've found in their small-group inquiry, we often ask the children to show us the one or two things they're most excited about in the different books they studied. If we feel they're ready, we might also ask them to do the envisioning part for us and tell us how they think someone in the room might try what they have found in his or her own illustrating. If they aren't able to do this independently, we make sure we do it for them. We want everything they find to be a concrete possibility someone might try.

FIGURE F.1 In his shark book, Josh uses an illustration technique in which something very large can exit off one page and enter onto the next (after the reader has turned the page). (1) What is this—is a shark coming? (2) Yes it is!

Another angle in thinking about illustrations that we've found useful during this study is to read the children a new picture book without showing them the illustrations. We talk first about what the book means with just the written words, then we go through it again with the illustrations and talk about how our meanings for it change. For example, *My Big Brother*, by Valorie Fisher (2002), is a good book for this because the illustrations add so much to the words. One page says, "He can do the most amazing things," and the accompanying illustration shows the big brother blowing bubbles with a bubble stick—not the "most amazing thing" most of us thought about when we read the words by themselves. As we talk about it, we realize one thing illustrations can do is make general words more specific by picturing what they really mean. So we say this in our discussion and then, as we do with *all* our talk around illustrations, we have to be sure to turn this into some thinking about our own writing. We envision someone doing this same thing in a book: "Helena might do this in one of her books about animals. The words might say, 'Some animals are very tricky' and her illustration could show a squirrel hanging upside down on a bird feeder."

During this study, we might also share with the children any information we can find about how illustrators make their decisions and what their processes are. For example, Katie and Lisa heard Chris Soentpiet speak at a conference once and learned that he sets up live models and props and takes photographs of the scenes he wants to paint for his books. In this study, we might tell children about this and then suggest someone could try doing this using our digital camera.

We don't have to hear illustrators in person to get this kind of information. Many picture books contain illustrators' notes that explain how the illustrations were created, and of course, we can find books, videos, and websites that have this sort of information as well. Our goal with information like this is that whatever we share with the children helps them envision new ways of going about their work as illustrators.

When we have a chart filled with possibilities we've found in books and learned from illustrators themselves, when we see the children trying all kinds of new moves in their own illustrations, and when the energy for the study begins to wane, we'll know it's time to move on. The directive "Tell me and show me what decisions you made in your illustrations" will become a standard assessment, and noticing what's happening in illustrations will be a part of all future studies, becoming more specific depending on what we're studying—illustrations in non-fiction texts, for example.

Resources for Getting Started

Because *every* picture book is filled with interesting things to notice about illustrations, we decided that instead of a book list, we would include a list of ten guiding questions for studying illustrations as resources for getting started. Remember that the point of pursuing all these questions is to come up with new visions for things our young writers might try in their picture books.

- How are the words and the illustrations laid out on the page in relation to one another? Is the layout consistent, or does it change from spread to spread? Is there anything particularly meaningful about the layout?

- What layout features are used in the text—borders, boxes, white space, labels, insets, and so on?

- How do the illustrations and the words work together to make meaning? Do the illustrations extend the meaning in any way?

- Is there anything happening in the illustrations that isn't happening in the words?

- What media was used to create the illustrations?

- Has the illustrator used color in any way to convey meaning in different illustrations?

- What are the different angles and focuses (zoomed in and out) of the illustrations? Do these relate to the meaning in any way?

- Do illustrations ever stand alone in the text? If so, how do they carry the meaning without words?

- Are there any words or print contained inside the illustrations themselves?

- Is there any manipulation of the print (size, color, font, left-to-right orientation) that is meaningful in the text?

How to Have Better Peer Conferences

Most young children surround much of their writing work with talk. Sometimes there is someone there to listen and sometimes there isn't, but it doesn't really matter anyway because often it's not a kind of talk that asks for any response. It's just talk. Sometimes they sing, too.

We understand this tendency—to narrate your thinking and actions with talk—to be natural in young children's work and, because we understand it, we do our best to embrace it (even when it gets a little noisy). We also try to teach *into* the talk, to help children understand ways they might use talk to help them make their books even better. This is what a study of peer conferring is all about with young children.

Figuring out our goals in a study like this has been a little journey of trial and error for us. Any illusions we had that we might help young children to internalize a reader's response and use that to help with drafting and revision were thwarted from the start. That might be a good goal for a study of peer conferring in, say, fourth grade, but we've found most six-year-olds joyfully and quite innocently don't really care that much about what other people think about their writing. They still live happily in their own egocentric worlds.

Once we realized this (we must have been having our nails done when they covered Piaget in our teacher training), we decided that the best way to teach them about peer conferencing would be to focus our study on the individual writer's needs—not on the response of a peer, but on what the writer could get out of this interaction. So, our main goal for a study like this is to help the children understand the kinds of help a writer might solicit from a peer and how to know when they need that help. However, an additional and very important goal for this study is that children will come to see soliciting help with writing as a good thing to do. So many of us learned in school (albeit not directly) that if we got help with something, particularly help that made the writing better, we were cheating somehow. We don't want our teaching to leave children with this stifling and untrue understanding about writing. We want them to know that all good writers get help—if not from a peer, then certainly from an editor—and that they can, too.

To help us figure out what we would teach about this, we relied mostly on what we know from our own experiences as writers getting help from our peers, the kinds of help we've noticed children *need* when they write, and some on what we know professional writers say about this. Using those resources, we settled on six kinds of conferences we would teach the children that they might seek out as they work on their writing. Our chart for the study looks like this:

HOW DO I KNOW WHEN I NEED A PEER CONFERENCE?

- I need some "wow!" in my writing.
- I'm just stuck.
- I have a question that I'm wondering about in my writing.
- I need to test-drive my piece.
- My ideas need to be bigger—ask me some questions.
- I need someone to look at my illustrations and make sure they match my text.

In this study, we'll use a fishbowl almost exclusively to help us teach. We'll begin each lesson with an explanation of the kind of conference we want to teach on that day, making as many connections as we can to the children's experiences as writers and times when we've seen they could have used this kind of help. Here, briefly, are explanations for each kind of conference:

- *I need some "wow!" in my writing* means that you want someone to look at what you're writing and help you think of some cool stuff—in the words and the illustrations—you might do to make the book really good.

- *I'm just stuck* means that you started writing and you can't think of anywhere else to go with it. You need to talk it out with someone until you get some more ideas and can carry on.

- *I have a question I'm wondering about in my writing* means there is something specific you want to ask someone about what you're writing. It may be a content question (Are birds mammals?) or it may be about the craft of the writing (Can you help me think of a good repeating line to use in this?).

- *I need to test-drive my piece* means you've written something and you think it's really funny or really sad or really disgusting or really *something*, and you need someone to read it so you can gauge the response. Does the reader laugh or seem sad or say "Oh gross!" after he has read it?

- *My ideas need to be bigger—ask me some questions* means you've gotten something written from beginning to end, but you know you need to make the ideas inside it bigger. You need someone to tell you what else she might like to know on each page.

- *I need someone to look at my illustrations and make sure they match the words on each page* means, well, exactly what it says! You want help thinking through your illustration decisions.

After the explanation, we'll then role-play that kind of conference in the fishbowl and have the children watch it and see what they notice. The role-play is usually one we've set up ahead of time so that the players know their roles and what's expected. We might use an actual piece from one of the children, or we might write our own piece to use during the role-play.

Once the conference in the fishbowl is over, we process it with the children. We make sure they've noticed important things such as how the two peers shared a look at the writing, the ways the help was asked for and given, the tone of the help, and the ways the writer made use of the help or kept track of the suggestions. We make sure the day's lesson ends with some envisioning. We think aloud with the children about what it would be like to be writing along one day, realize they need this kind of help with their writing, and then go and seek it out from one of their classmates. We often end these lessons with a request that they let us know if they have a conference like this with someone so that we can talk about how it went for them during share time.

Because this is actually a study that supports the writing process, we may embed some teaching from professional authors along the way in this series of lessons. We might share with the children a quote we've found (from a writer they know) about working with other writers and then help them make meaning for their own writing work from this quote.

At the end of this study, we expect to see children using their new visions for peer conferences to help them talk more productively as they're writing. We'll want to watch for this and comment on it and teach into the problems we see that emerge from it. We'll expect that the children might invent new ways to help each other through talk, and we'll watch for this too and add their inventions to our chart, sometimes long after the official study is over. "Did you get any help from any other writers with this?" will become a predictable question in our assessment from this point forward.

Literary Nonfiction

What is this genre, exactly? Actually, that label could apply to lots of kinds of writing in the world, so let's describe, instead, what's in our stack in this study. What particular kind of literary nonfiction are we going to study? First, let's list just ten books (there would be more than this) that very likely would be in this stack. For our youngest writers, they are all picture books.

Atlantic. 2002. G. Brian Karas.

Bat Loves the Night. 2001. Nicola Davies, illus. by Sarah Fox-Davies.

Big Blue Whale. 1997. Nicola Davies, illus. by Nick Maland.

Cave. 2000. Diane Siebert, illus. by Wayne McLoughlin.

I Call It Sky. 1999. Will C. Howell, illus. by John Ward.

If You Were Born a Kitten. 1997. Marion Dane Bauer, illus. by JoEllen McAllister Stammen.

River Story. 2000. Meredith Hooper, illus. by Bee Willey.

Salamander Rain: A Lake and Pond Journal. 2000. Kristin Joy Pratt-Serafini.

Supermarket. 2001. Kathleen Krull, illus. by Melanie Hope Greenberg.

When Hunger Calls. 1994. Bert Kitchen.

What all these books have in common is that they engage and entertain us as readers, but they also inform us about a topic. In other words, they teach us some facts but also create an interesting context around those facts. In this study, this is the kind of thing we are going to try to write.

There are several things that are interesting about this stack of books we are going to study. They are all picture books, but the written text inside most of them is more sophisticated—especially in terms of length and depth—than what most of our youngest writers will actually produce. Of course, this has been true of much of the writing we've studied across the year. Many of the children won't even be able to read all these books independently and will have to rely on our reading them aloud during the study. So how is it that this is an appropriate stack of texts for our study? It's appropriate because we'll be focusing on the *craft* of this writing, looking at the different ways these authors and illustrators have approached the writing of this genre and seeing what they've tried in a variety of books that we might also try.

Take Kristin Joy Pratt-Serafini's *Salamander Rain: A Lake and Pond Journal*, for example. It's actually a very sophisticated, complex text with lots of information embedded in both the words and the pictures. We don't expect the children to create an actual text of this complexity, but as we study it together, we do expect them to come away with some very specific visions of things they might try in their books of this type. From this particular book, these visions might include

- One way I could write this genre is to make my book actually look like someone's journal with lots of notes and pictures and little collected things taped into it.

- I could create characters and a setting and a story line and use them to get at my facts.

- I might use borders in my illustrations that contain pictures and labels related to my topic.

- I could use boxes to set off some specific facts I want to throw in throughout the book.

- I could have pictures that are labeled, maps, and scales for sizing things in my book.

- I could have a list of other books and websites about my topic that readers might want to check out.

Any of our youngest writers could try some or all of these writing techniques if they wanted to use them in the books they're writing (remember, they will look like six-year-olds trying them). This is especially true if we spend some time envisioning what it would look or sound like if one of them tried something here. It's this focus on technique that makes the writing in the books we study accessible to the young writers we teach.

For our youngest writers, we'll stay focused on one big goal in this study: we want the children to see a range of options for how they might *approach* this kind of writing. "How might we write books that are fun to read but also teach readers about something?" will be our guiding question. With each book we study, we'll consider how the factual information is included in the text, because this is one of the central issues faced by a writer of this genre. This will get us looking at text features such as labeled pictures, maps, and charts.

To help make clear what we mean by the approach to the writing, let's consider the nine other books on the previous list. If we stay focused on big ways to approach the writing of this genre, here are some of the kinds of techniques we'd likely have on our chart after studying them closely:

WAYS TO APPROACH THE WRITING OF LITERARY NONFICTION

Atlantic

- I could write about something by giving it a voice and letting it speak in first person.

- I could include a list of facts about my topic at the end of my book.

Bat Loves the Night

- I could write about something in present tense like it's happening as you are reading it. If I write about it in third person, it's like you are watching it happen.

- I could embed facts (that relate to my running story) *around* my illustrations.

Big Blue Whale

- I could ask my reader to do things with direct commands in my book ("Look into its eye. . . .")

- I could embed facts (that relate to my running story) *around* my illustrations.

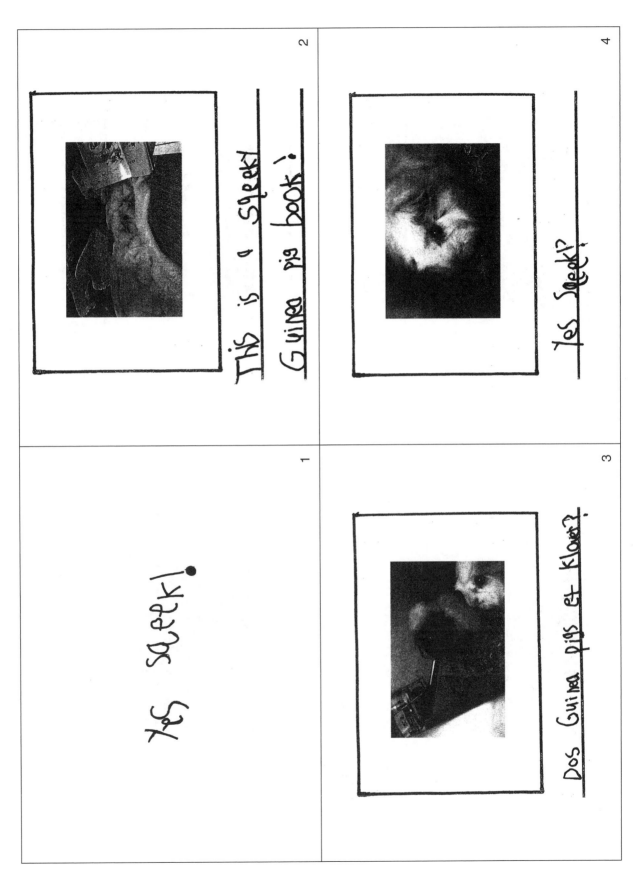

FIGURE H.1 A very beginning writer uses a playful question-and-answer structure to write about guinea pigs. (1) Yes squeak! (2) This is a squeaky guinea pig book! (3) Do guinea pigs eat clover? (4) Yes squeak!

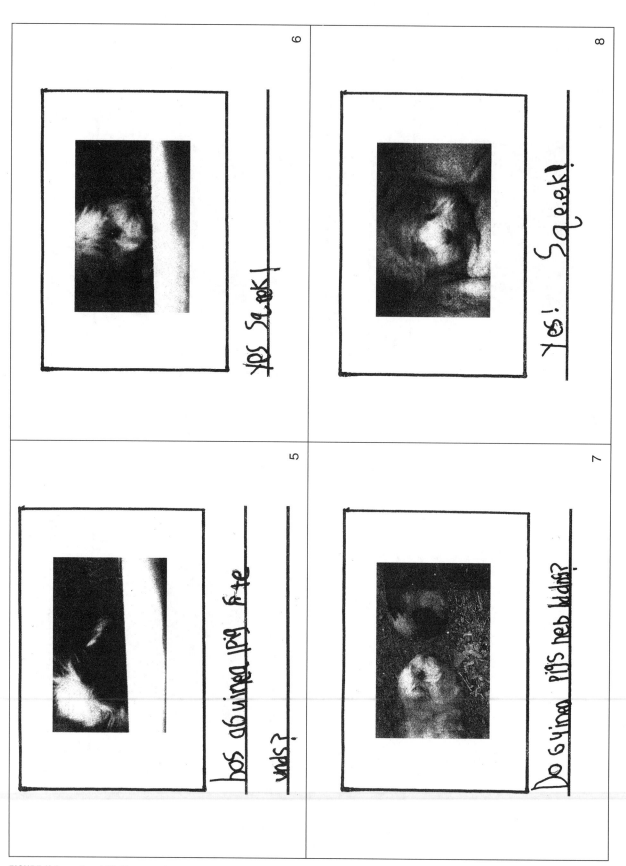

FIGURE H.1 *continued* (5) Does a guinea pig _____ ? (6) Yes squeak! (7) Do guinea pigs need bedding? (8) Yes! Squeak!

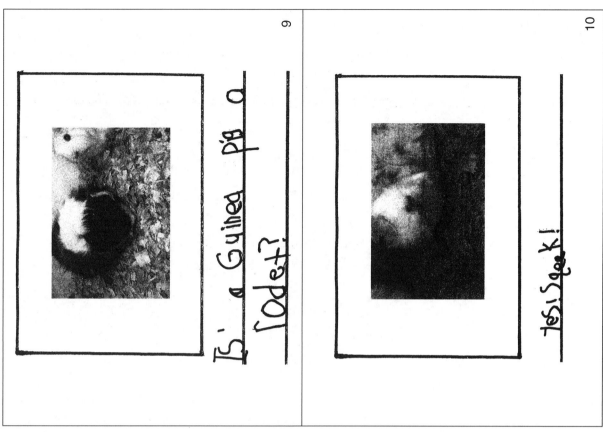

FIGURE H.1 *continued* (9) Is a guinea pig a rodent? (10) Yes! Squeak!

Cave

- I could write my book so it looks and sounds like poetry.

- I could have an author's note at the end of my book that gives more facts about my topic.

I Call It Sky

- I could write in first person about my topic and share my own experience with it.

- I could use an afterword to share more facts about the topic of my book.

If You Were Born a Kitten

- I could write my book as a whole series of "if, then" propositions for my reader to think about. I'd use the second-person pronoun *you* to engage my reader.

- My facts could be embedded right in my main text (not set apart in any way).

River Story

- I could write about my topic by following it through time and/or place.

- I could include a summarizing illustration at the end of my book with more facts embedded around it.

Supermarket

- I could write my book as a list of things I know about my topic.

- I could embed related facts *into* my illustrations.

When Hunger Calls

- I could write my book as a series of vignettes and start each new one with a repeated phrase related to my topic to tie them together.

- My facts could be embedded right in my main text (not set apart in any way).

When we look at a chart like this, we are always struck with how abstract these visions for writing seem if you haven't looked closely at these books and been a part of the conversations with the children that generated them. They come to life when we talk about them and especially when we envision someone in the class writing about one of his or her own topics in these ways. That part is just so critical, as we've said again and again throughout this book.

We also know that a chart like this simply captures our focus for the study. We actually find ourselves having lots of conversations about other crafting techniques (word choice, structure, punctuation, illustrations, layout, leads, endings, titles, etc.) we see writers using in these books, especially when this study happens later in the year. We stand on the shoulders of earlier studies and can't help but notice writers using language in many of the same ways we've seen them use it in our other studies.

One thing we have had to be careful about in our study of this kind of writing is making sure we have a good variety of topics represented in our stack of books. In our early studies of this kind of writing, we found that many children came away from the study thinking that literary nonfiction was writing about animals. And though this was never an intention in our teaching, we realized that our animal-heavy stack of examples conveyed this message to them. Since we learned that lesson, we have tried to be quite intentional in helping the children understand that literary nonfiction can be about any topic of interest to a writer as

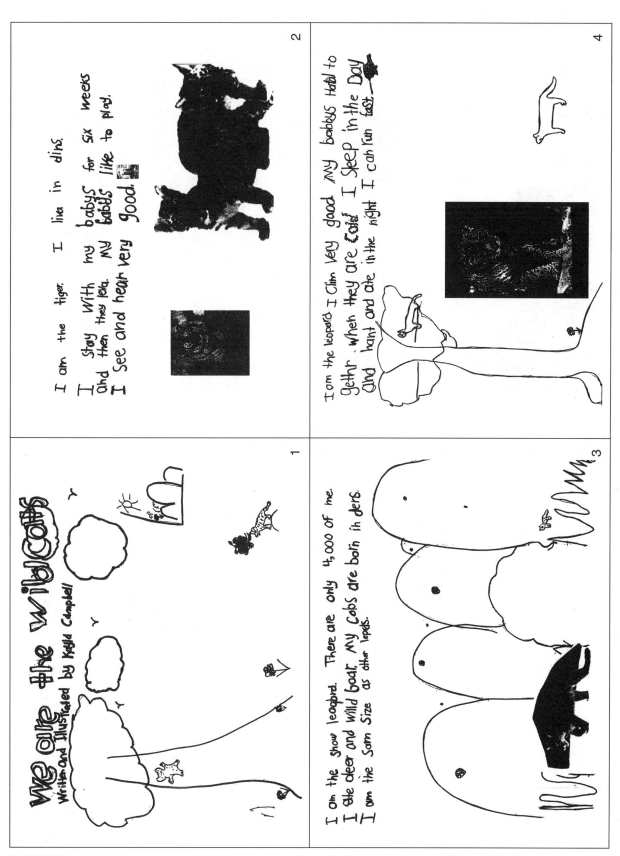

FIGURE H.2 Kayla uses a first-person voice to let a series of animals speak in *We Are the Wildcats*. She ends her book with labeled pictures. (2) I am the tiger. I live in dens. I stay with my babies for six weeks and then they leave. My babies like to play. I see and hear very good. (3) I am the snow leopard. There are only 4,000 of me. I eat deer and wild boar. My cubs are born in dens. I am the same size as other leopard. (4) I am the leopard. I climb very good. My babies huddle together when they are cold. I sleep in the day and hunt and eat in the night. I can run fast.

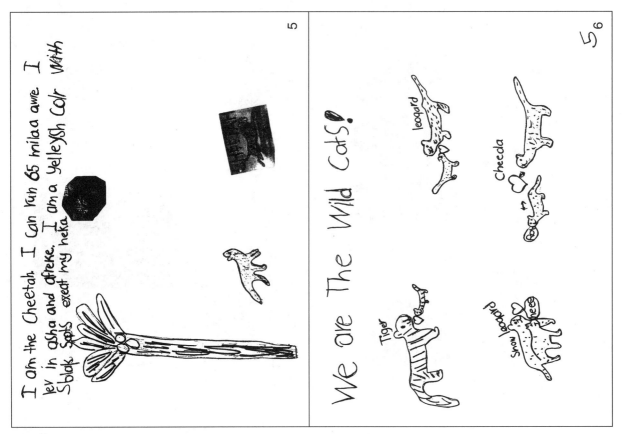

FIGURE H.2 *continued* (5) I am the cheetah. I can run 65 miles an hour. I am a yellowish color with black spots. (6) We are the wild cats!

long as the writer has some information or insight to share with others. We still find that many of them choose to write about animals in their own literary nonfiction and we believe the explanation for this is quite simple: animals interest them.

During the course of this study, we expect, of course, that children will write literary nonfiction and use some of the approaches to this kind of writing that they've learned in our study. We also expect to see them *working* like writers of literary nonfiction during writing workshop, and we teach into this expectation. We help them find books and websites they might use for research. We might show them how to use tools such as interviews, surveys, and observations for research. Sometimes we introduce them to small writers' notebooks in which they can write down interesting information about their topics that they might use in their writing. We encourage them to check the accuracy of their facts.

We find the study of literary nonfiction to be such a natural study for our youngest writers. They love spending time with these kinds of books. They pore over the same illustrations again and again and surprise each other with interesting facts they find. They love joining the club of people who write these books, and we love initiating them into that club.

FIGURE H.3 Hunter chooses a topic *other* than animals for his piece about Fontana Lake. His approach is to write in first person so the lake speaks. (1) I am the lake. (2) People race their boats on me and when they race their boats on me it tickles. (3) People fish on me. (4) Fish live in me.

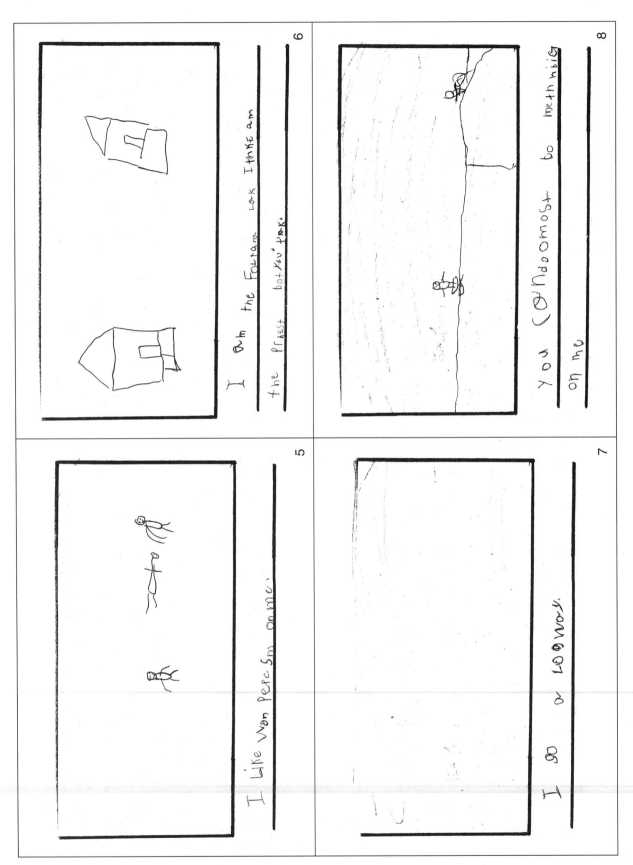

FIGURE H.3 *continued* (5) I like when people swim on me. (6) I am the Fontana Lake. I think (I) am the prettiest. Don't you think? (7) I go a long way. (8) You can almost do many things on me.

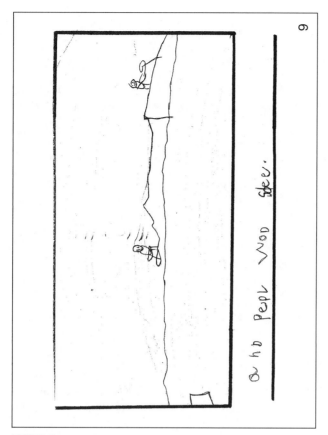

FIGURE H.3 *continued* (9) And people water ski.

Resources for Getting Started

The following is a list of twenty other books to use to show our youngest writers possibilities for ways to approach the writing of this genre.

> *Animal Dads.* 1997. Sneed B. Collard III, illus. by Steve Jenkins.
>
> *A Desert Scrapbook: Dawn to Dusk in the Sonoran Desert.* 1998. Virginia Wright–Frierson.
>
> *Do They Scare You?* 1992. Sneed B. Collard III, illus. by Kristin Kest.
>
> *Dream Weaver.* 1998. Jonathan London, illus. by Rocco Baviera.
>
> *Eaglet's World.* 2002. Evelyn Minshull, illus. by Andrea Gabriel.
>
> *Elephants Swim.* 1995. Linda Capus Riley, illus. by Steve Jenkins.
>
> *Families of the Deep Blue Sea.* 1995. Kenneth Mallory, illus. by Marshall Peck III.
>
> *Gentle Giant Octopus.* 1998. Karen Wallace, illus. by Mike Bostock.

My Favorite Bear. 2003. Andrea Gabriel.

No One Told the Aardvark. 1997. Deborah Eaton and Susan Halter, illus. by Jim Spense.

On the River ABC. 1993. Caroline Stutson, illus. by Anna-Maria L. Crum.

One Tiny Turtle. 2001. Nicola Davies, illus. by Jane Chapman.

Red-Eyed Tree Frog. 1999. Joy Cowley, photos by Nic Bishop.

Somewhere Today. 1992. Bert Kitchen.

Sophie Skates. 1999. Rachel Isadora.

Tiger Trail. 2000. Kay Winters, illus. by Laura Regan.

A Walk in the Rainforest. 1992. Kristin Joy Pratt.

Walk with a Wolf. 1997. Janni Howker, illus. by Sarah Fox-Davies.

Water Dance. 1997. Thomas Locker.

The World Is Full of Babies: How All Sorts of Babies Grow and Develop. 1996. Mick Manning and Brita Granström.

How to Use Punctuation in Interesting Ways

In the introduction to her wonderful book *A Fresh Approach to Teaching Punctuation* (2002), Janet Angelillo says, "Writers use punctuation to shape the way readers read their texts. The system of little symbols we know as punctuation is full of meaning, nuance, and intricacy. It helps writing make sense to readers; it allows us to control the pace and volume and rhythm of the words. Used wisely, it is an invaluable writing tool" (8). This unit of study is meant to introduce our youngest writers to this invaluable writing tool and to nudge them to use punctuation in thoughtful, interesting ways in the texts they create.

Depending on when in the school year this study occurs, students may have already done a good bit of talking and thinking about punctuation as they've looked at texts for a variety of other reasons. They can't help but notice it, especially if they're reading like writers, because it's such a big part of how writers craft their texts. Also, as beginning readers, they have lots of experience thinking about how punctuation is meant to guide their reading. In this series of lessons, we simply want to turn our full attention to this aspect of written texts and think very specifically about how we can *use* punctuation.

Usually, by the time this study occurs, we have also done a lot of work with the children around the most basic, mechanical aspects of punctuation, namely, end marks for sentences and the capitalization that goes with the end marks. We've demonstrated how these work again and again in that all-day-long teaching that wraps its arms around the writing workshop and we've also helped children with them during individual writing conferences. This unit of study is meant to push beyond the bounds of these basic mechanics of punctuation and really look at other kinds of marks writers use in intentional (as opposed to mechanical) ways to "control the pace and volume and rhythm of the words."

Our goal for this study is that children will begin using some different punctuation marks in intentional ways. As you probably can anticipate by now, we don't have a specific set of marks we want to cover and master during the study. In our minilessons we will dive back into texts, pay attention to the punctuation we see, and come to some understandings about the potential of different marks—commas, colons, ellipses, semicolons, parentheses, and so on. During the study we are also likely to talk about other tools a writer may use to cause a text to be read a particular way—using bold or italic print or capital letters, for example. In the minilessons, we'll make sure we always end with envisioning how the children might use these different tools in their own writing, then we'll send them out to write in a room that's filling up with new possibilities for punctuation use.

One thing that may be surprising is that we are not overly concerned that students use punctuation in textbook, "right" ways when they begin experimenting with it. At this developmental stage in their writing lives, we are concerned more that they are purposeful when they use it and that their theories about why they are using punctuation make sense, even if they are not quite conventional. We know that as they get more experience with punctuation—as writers and as readers—they will gain more control of it. But as they gain this control, we hope they never lose the sense of purpose about punctuation that we want them to gain from this study. Interestingly enough, many of us were taught when we were in school that *all* punctuation use was mechanical, and that because of that, we had no real decisions to make when we used it. Our only sense of purpose was to get it right; we never learned what all successful writers know: that punctuation is a tool to be used. We want our students to come away from this study with a very clear sense of this.

In this series of minilessons we will return to many books we know and we'll likely introduce some new ones. We'll try to choose books that we know have a variety of punctuation marks being used in interesting ways. With these books, we will show students some punctuation moves, walk through others and ask the children what they notice about the punctuation, and then have them do some small-group inquiry and find interesting uses of punctuation on their own. Our class chart will fill quickly with specific marks we like, different examples of them being used, and simple, usable explanations of how they work. After studying

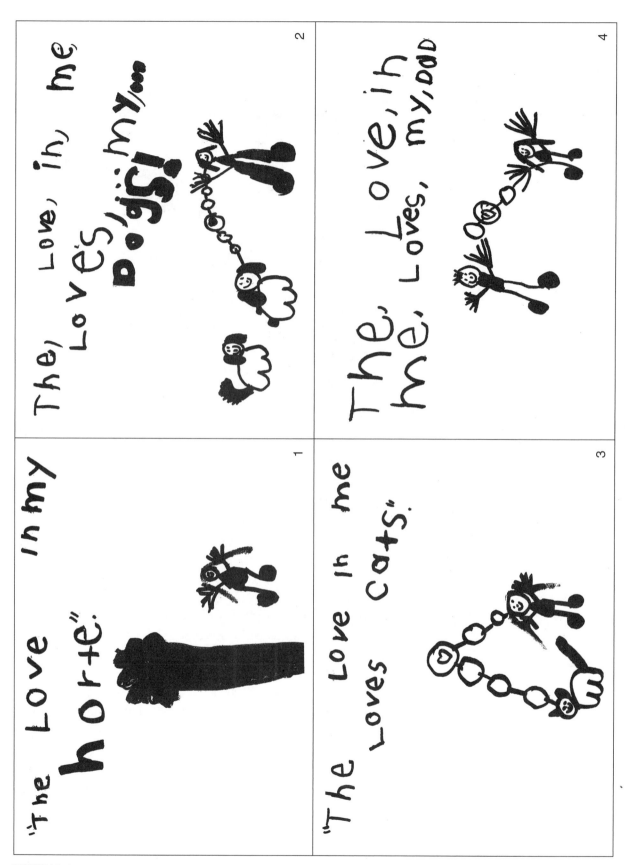

FIGURE I.1 A young writer experiments with punctuation. When she reads what she's written, it's clear she knows what work each mark is supposed to do in her text.

The love. in
me loves
my mom!

5

FIGURE I.1 *continued*

The Wonderful Happens (2000), by Cynthia Rylant, for example, we might make an entry on our chart that looks like this:

> **Colon:** It can set you up for a surprise word to follow it—you wonder what it will be. Ex: "the earth grew wheat, the wheat made flour, and the wonderful happened: bread."

When we envision someone in the room using a mark in this way, we often physically write an example. This is different from lots of our envisioning, when we write our examples aloud but not on paper. We do this with punctuation because punctuation is all about how it looks on the page. So on the day when we talk about using a colon, we might write an example like this:

> When Cassie opened her present, she couldn't believe what was inside: a new Barbie.

As we look at more books over time, we'll find other uses of specific marks that work just like our originals, and usually we'll find examples where the marks are used in other ways. These will require a new entry on our chart as we discover a new potential for a specific mark. Before long, we almost always discover that some punctuation marks can do the same work in a text. A dash, for example, could have been used instead of a colon in the example from *The Wonderful Happens*. Once we begin to notice these overlapping purposes, we'll begin to nudge the children to think of other decisions a writer could have made for how to punctuate something. This thinking will further deepen their understanding that punctuating a text is a decision-making process.

One thing seems worth noting here. We don't shy away from looking at books that have some very alternative uses for punctuation. As a matter of fact, we embrace books like this because we think they help children understand that idea of purposeful use that matters so much to us. In *The Wonderful Happens*, for example, someone has made a very interesting decision *not* to capitalize the first words in all the sentences throughout the text. We look at this and we talk about why that decision might have been made. We don't talk about it being *wrong*; we talk about it being someone's *decision* to do something unconventionally. And we should say, this is really how we see it; we're not just explaining it this way to be friendly to small children.

Reading aloud well will be so critical in this study. As we're looking at books and trying to understand how punctuation is being used, we will really emphasize how the punctuation causes us to read the text in a particular way. Out of this emphasis, we will also do some strategy lessons that show children how to look at their own writing and figure out what punctuation they will need based on how they want the writing to sound when it's read. When children read us their work, we'll make sure they are reading it as it is punctuated and help them figure out whether the punctuation decisions they've made are working well in their texts.

Along these same lines, we might look at some books that are *very* dependent on the punctuation for meaning, books like Chris Raschka's companions *Yo! Yes?* (1998) and *Ring! Yo?* (2000) We'll cover the punctuation marks somehow and then play around with trying different marks in different places to see their impact on meaning and sound. This kind of work helps children realize how much weight a single mark can carry in certain situations. We'll want to be sure to envision this happening in their writing—a punctuation mark being very weighty—before we get out of these lessons.

While students will likely begin using punctuation more purposefully right from the start of this study, we may want to require them all to write at least one piece (in any genre) that really shows them using punctuation in a very purposeful way. We certainly will make questions

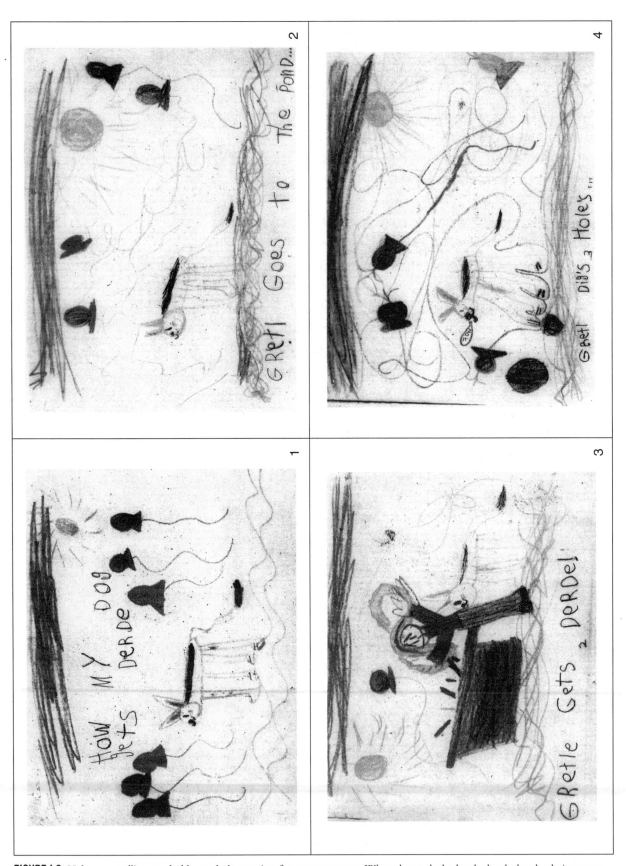

FIGURE I.2 Helena uses ellipses to hold a reader's attention from page to page. When she reads the book aloud, she clearly intonates the ellipses by raising the pitch of the last syllable in the word just before the marks. (1) How my dog gets dirty. (2) Gretle goes to the pond . . . (3) Gretle gets dirty! (4) Gretle digs holes . . .

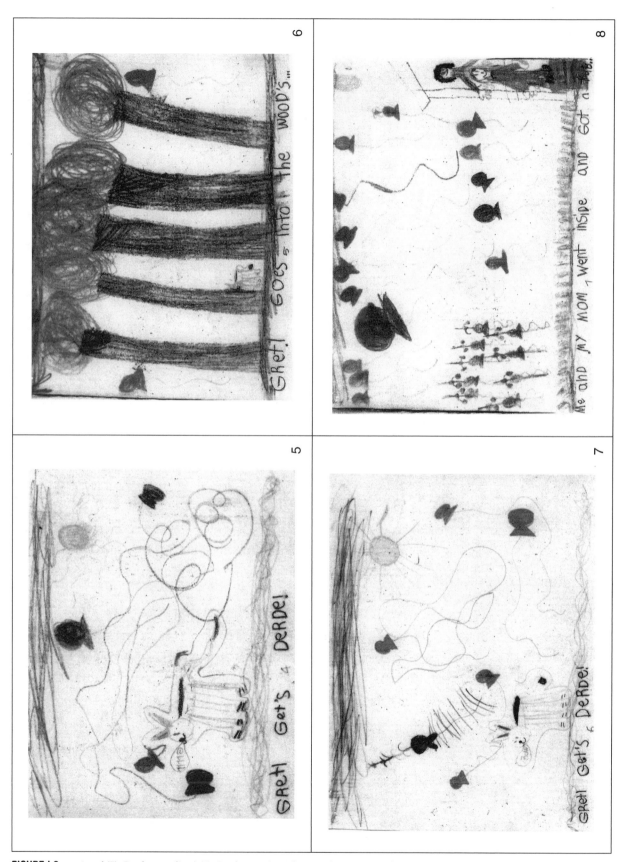

FIGURE I.2 *continued* (5) Gretle gets dirty! (6) Gretle goes into the woods . . . (7) Gretle gets dirty! (8) Me and my mom went inside and got a tub . . .

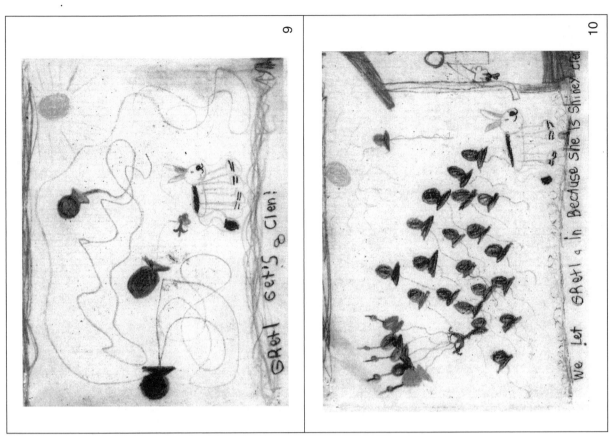

9

10

FIGURE I.2 *continued* (9) Gretl gets clean! (10) We let Gretl in because she is shiny clean!

about punctuation a standard part of our assessment after this study, and we'll expect to continue to talk about it when we notice writers using it in interesting ways in the new texts we encounter along the way.

Resources for Getting Started

Here is a starter list of ten good books appropriate for our youngest writers. Each one has a variety of interesting uses of punctuation and examples of other tools a writer may use to cause a text to be read a particular way (bold or italic print, capital letters, etc.).

Click, Clack, Moo: Cows That Type. 2000. Doreen Cronin, illus. by Betsy Lewin.

Eaglet's World. 2002. Evelyn Minshull, illus. by Andrea Gabriel.

Hoptoad. 2003. Jane Yolen, illus. by Karen Lee Schmidt.

If You See a Kitten. 2002. John Butler.

Little One Step. 2003. Simon James.

My Grandmother's Clock. 2002. Geraldine McCaughrean, illus. by Stephen Lambert.

Once There Was a Bull . . . (frog). 1995. Rick Walton, illus. by Greg Hally.

Roller Coaster. 2003. Marla Frazee.

Sail Away. 1995. Donald Crews.

Trucks. Whizz! Zoom! Rumble! 2003. Patricia Hubbell, illus. by Megan Halsey.

Poetry

In a genre study of poetry, we have just a few simple goals for our youngest writers. First, we want them to understand that poetry is a form of writing they can use to actually say something meaningful about all their many interests and passions in life. We want to make sure they know that writing a poem is not simply a process of finding some words that rhyme and then piecing them together, a belief many of them have because of their limited experiences with poetry. For this reason, throughout the study we'll make sure they are exposed extensively to poems that don't rhyme.

Another goal we have is for the children to see poetry as the stuff of everyday life. We want to immerse them in poems about ordinary things and experiences and, in doing so, help them see that potential poems are all around them. Early in the study as we're reading these poems, we'll share great quotes from poets on how they get ideas from all around them. As we think with the children about how poets must move through the world finding ideas for poems everywhere, we'll go out on poetry walks together. We'll also ask often, "Did any of you get a great idea for a poem while you were out in the world after school yesterday?"

We might use a modified version of a small writer's notebook during this study and encourage the children to write down little notes about things they see that they might make into poems. When we do use notebooks of this kind, we'll need a few minilessons to show the students how to turn their notes into poems. However, one thing we have found is that lots of the children actually write their notebook en-

> ### I Hear Nature
>
> I hear nature
> everywhere I go.
> I hear the wind
> blowing hard.
> I hear the squishy
> noise from the wet
> muddy ground.
> I hear the beautiful
> birds singing.
> I hear nature.
>
> —*Helena Hunt, 2002*

FIGURE J.1 Helena writes a poem from her observations after a poetry walk.

tries as poems rather than as notes. Developmentally, writing it one way (as notes) so you can go back and write it another way later (as a poem) requires a kind of thinking into the future that some of them don't seem ready to do. We recognize this and accept that some of them will use the notebook in this approximated way.

Another goal of the study related to topic choice is for the children to see that poetry is one way writers often approach a broad topic. Instead of writing a single poem about fishing, in other words, a poet might write a whole collection of poems about fishing. To help them understand this, we are careful to choose lots of collections of poems that are written by a single poet about a specific topic.

As we immerse ourselves in reading poems from a variety of collections, we find year after year that three main features of poetry tend to come up again and again: line breaks, white space, and specific word choices. These features have now become a focus for us in this study. We know there is lots more to know about this wonderful genre, but we feel this is a good starting place for our youngest writers. We want them to think a lot about choosing just a few words and then getting them down on the page so they look like a poem. In addition to these features, we also talk a lot about punctuation in a poetry study. The children are usually fascinated by how writers often use this tool in different ways (from prose) in this genre.

We'll also do a lot of work in this study with teaching the children to read their poems well, to read them so they sound like poems. We want them to know that even when a poem doesn't rhyme, the poet still

Be quiet and think that you're in a place with
lots of beautiful flowers
Daisylions all around you.
You just fall as the roses tickle your face
As you look at the clouds and...see to you that
the clouds look like
Tulips
As you fall!

-Jared Rigdon
4/2/02

FIGURE J.2 First, Jared jotted a note in his notebook about "daisylions." Next, he drafted a poem. Then he fancy published it on the computer. (1) I see two daisy lions-four died out daisy lions. (2) Flowers / Be quiet and / think that you're / in a place with / lots of beautiful / flowers daisy lions / all around you / you just fall / as the roses tickle / your face as / you look at the / clouds and see to you / that the clouds / look like tulips / as you fall.

pays a lot of attention to the sound of words and how they work together in the poem. To this end, we'll ask them over and over to listen to how the poems we read aloud sound, and we'll have them read their poems aloud over and over until it's clear they are really focusing on the words they've chosen sounding like poetry. We'll also try to help them see that how the poem goes down on the page has a lot to do with the way readers approach the reading of it, and then we'll nudge them to be sure their decisions about this match the way they want their poems to be read.

We'll follow all the same predictable patterns of teaching in this study as we do in our other studies of this type. We'll collect a good stack of poetry anthologies—most of them will be picture books—that we believe will give our students a good vision for the potential of poetry. We'll immerse ourselves in reading poems. Sometimes we'll read a whole anthology in one sitting, as this helps the children see how a collection of poems can go together around a topic. We'll start by pointing out a few things to the children in the poems we've been reading, and then we'll quickly move to asking them to notice how poems are written, and we'll build our content from what they notice.

Stars

Now it is
night.
The stars are
twinkling
while I sleep.
I love to
watch them
twinkle.
They are bright
and so tiny
but in space
they are BIG
they glow
so big and
shine so tiny.

—Ashley McClure 4-2-2002

FIGURE J.3 The delightful surprise that poetry sometimes brings—*they glow so big and shine so tiny*—is evident in Ashley's poem.

One thing that is a little different in this study is how we envision the techniques of poetry we are finding as we read and notice together. We find that we must actually write down on chart paper a lot of what we envision with the children, rather than writing it aloud as we do in many studies. This is because so much of our focus in the study is on how poems go down on the page with line breaks and white space. You may remember that we do a lot of this in a punctuation study for the same reason—we need to see how what we're envisioning might look on the page.

Noticeably absent from our study of poetry are formulas for writing single poems—bio poems and "I am . . ." poems and the like. These formulas may help someone write a single poem (albeit a poem a lot like everyone else's poem), but they don't help children come to understand the *genre* of poetry and all the techniques writers use to write in this form. We want our children to learn from real poets how to write poems, and the formulaic poems, while they line the halls of many schools, don't really exist in the world of literature outside of school. So, the poems our children write are a little more all over the place than they would be if we gave them formulas, but the understandings the children use to write these poems are deep and true and will lead them, we hope, to more poetry in their futures as writers.

Most of the children begin writing poems right away in this study. We'll put a big emphasis on sharing these poems often during the study because we want children reading them aloud and hearing them read aloud, and we want to get a really good pool of ideas in the room for the kinds of things children are trying in their poems. We'll put a lot of their poems up around the room right away and encourage the children to visit them and read and reread them to themselves and to each other. Because we want them reading the poems, we'll actually publish a lot of these on the computer so the spelling is easier to read. We also find that the interaction around typing a poem up on the computer is a good teaching opportunity if we are there when it happens (sometimes we let the children do it on their own). Many of the children like to play with different options for the line breaks and the white space they create and with capitalization, punctuation, and font as their poems are being typed ·up, and we can help them think through their decision making as they do this if we're there.

Resources for Getting Started

The following is a list of twenty poetry anthologies that are appropriate for our youngest writers and help give them the visions for poetry that we outlined in this section.

Advice for a Frog. 1995. Alice Schertle, illus. by Norman Green.

Candy Corn. 1999. James Stevenson.

Earthmates. 2000. Patricia Hubbell, illus. by Jean Cassels.

Flicker Flash. 1999. Joan Bransfield Graham, illus. by Nancy Davis.

From the Bellybutton of the Moon / Del Ombligo de la Luna. 1998. Francisco X. Alarcón, illus. by Maya Christina Gonzales.

Give Yourself to the Rain. 2002. Margaret Wise Brown, illus. by Teri L. Weidner.

Hey You! C'mere—A Poetry Slam. 2002. Elizabeth Swados, illus. by Joe Cepeda.

Horizons: Poems as Far as the Eye Can See. 2002. Jane Yolen, illus. by Jason Stemple (see also their other collaborations *Water Music; Once upon Ice; Snow, Snow*).

Isn't My Name Magical? Sister and Brother Poems. 1999. James Berry, illus. by Shelly Hehenberger.

It's Raining Laughter. 1997. Nikki Grimes, illus. by Myles C. Pinkney.

January Rides the Wind. 1997. Charlotte F. Otten, illus. by Todd L. W. Doney.

Little Dog Poems. 1999. Kristine O'Connell George, illus. by June Otani.

A Lucky Thing. 1999. Alice Schertle, illus. by Wendell Minor.

Lunch Money and Other Poems About School. 1995. Carol Diggory Shields, illus. by Paul Meisel.

Night Garden: Poems from the World of Sleep. 2000. Janet S. Wong, illus. by Julia Paschkis.

Perfect Harmony: A Musical Journey with the Boys Choir of Harlem. 2002. Charles R. Smith Jr. (see also *Short Takes: Fast Break Basketball Poetry*).

Silver Seeds. 2001. Paul Paolilli and Dan Brewer, illus. by Steve Johnson and Lou Fancher.

Sitting Pretty: A Celebration of Black Dolls. 2000. Dinah Johnson, illus. by Myles C. Pinkney.

Sky Words. 1994. Marilyn Singer, illus. by Deborah Kogan Ray.

Toasting Marshmallows: Camping Poems. 2001. Kristine O'Connell George, illus. by Kate Kiesler (see also their other collaborations *The Great Frog Race* and *Old Elm Speaks: Tree Poems*).

Revision

While we'll talk some as a whole class and some with individual children about revision across the year in what we hope are developmentally appropriate ways, we have found a short, focused study of revision near the end of the year to be a worthwhile process study. For our youngest writers we'll focus the study on just one kind of revision: adding detail to a text to make it fuller and more meaningful. Focusing on this type of revision makes sense to us because so many of the children write these wonderful, often tightly structured, but *short* texts—especially early in the year when their stamina hasn't built up a lot yet. These pieces are ripe for additive revision, and adding on to something is a very concrete way to approach revision when you are just beginning to understand what the process entails. We know full well that by late in second grade, when they go through that volume-is-everything phase and want to write very long pieces, revision as taking out and moving around will need to be the focus of our teaching. Later, revision as re-thinking and actually changing what's in a text will be layered in as an important understanding. But in first grade, adding on just makes sense as a beginning place.

There are a number of ways this study might go, but we'll walk through our latest version of it just to give a feel for one way it could go.

We'll begin the study with some teaching from our own writing and some appropriate quotes from professional writers about what revision means in the whole process of writing. Our goal will be to help children realize—in a very beginning way—that most writers revisit things they have written and try their hand at doing something to make the writing better. They are often impressed to hear some of the big numbers of drafts writers say they do. Valerie Worth, whose small poems they love, for example, says, "In many cases I work on a very short poem for months. I have done hundreds of revisions for a single poem" (Copeland 1993, 74).

After a few lessons on what revision is, we'll ask the children to choose a book that they've written during the year and like so much that they want to revisit it and try some revision on it (we're going to work only with prose in this study, not poetry). Notice that right away we are trying to communicate an important message about revision: It's not something you do because you messed up or didn't do things right the first time. Revision is something writers do because they love something they're writing so much, they want to keep playing with its potential. A big goal for us in this study is to help our youngest writers begin to develop healthy attitudes about revision.

One thing we've learned along the way is that we sometimes need to guide the children a little as they decide on a piece to revisit. Because we are going to focus on revision as adding on to a piece, they need to choose something that has real potential for more volume. Sometimes they choose pieces they love, but they're really not ones they have a lot more to say about, and the revision ends up not really making the piece any better. That's what happened to Cassey when she chose the book *Shoes* to revise. She loved this book (and so did her teachers), but there just wasn't a lot more to say that would make this simple list book better (see Figure K.1). We learned from this that if we can help the children choose a piece where we know they have a lot more to say, then the revision work will go more smoothly for them and they'll come to better understandings about what the work can mean to their writing.

Once the students have chosen a piece they want to revise, we need to decide on a manageable way for them to do this work. We don't want to overburden them with rewriting all they've already written. Taking a cue from our friend and fellow teacher Isoke Nia, we decided to quickly type the children's books up for them and leave spaces for them to add to each page. Another option would be to use large sticky notes for making the additions.

As we're preparing their books for this revision work, we'll teach a series of minilessons on kinds of things writers might add to make a piece fuller and more meaningful:

- talk—something someone might have said
- descriptive detail about what things look, smell, sound, feel, or taste like
- specific detail for general things ("lots of presents" becomes "hula hoop, a skateboard, Legos™, and a new Harry Potter book")

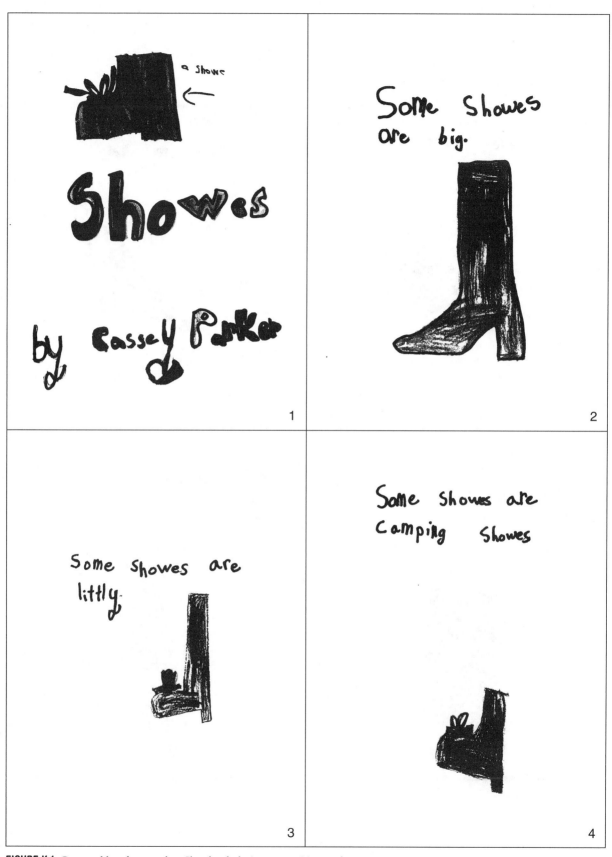

FIGURE K.1 Cassey adds volume to her *Shoes* book during our revision study.

FIGURE K.1 *continued*

Shoes
By Cassey Parker

Some shoes are big.

Some Shoes are big because they dont fet on My feet.

Some shoes are little.

Some shoes are little because they hert my feet.

Some shoes are camping shoes.

Some shoes are camping shoes because they dont hert my feet on rokes.

9

Some shoes are purple.

Some shoes are parple because they are.

Some shoes are cowgirl shoes.

Some shoes are cowgirl shoes because you can ride on your hoese.

All shoes go on your feet.

All shoes go on your feet or you get bee shengea lue?

10

FIGURE K.1 *continued*

- more information (if it's factual)
- action—something else happens

As we introduce each of these, we'll have some writing we can use to show how to add this kind of information. We might write a piece to use as an example, or we might use some of their work that they didn't choose to use on their own. The two pages in Figure K.2 are some of the ones Katie used in these minilessons. They show examples of adding action, visual detail, specific detail, and some talk. Notice that she is using the same format to make these revisions that she'll have the students use to make their revisions. Envisioning is just as important in these minilessons as it is in any other lesson. As we focus on a kind of addition, we envision one of the children adding something like that to a book he or she has written and we write (out loud) what it would sound like.

Just before we send the children out to do their revisions, we'll likely show them how to work together, if they want, to think of what they might add page by page. We might use a fishbowl to show an example of one writer helping another in this way and then process that

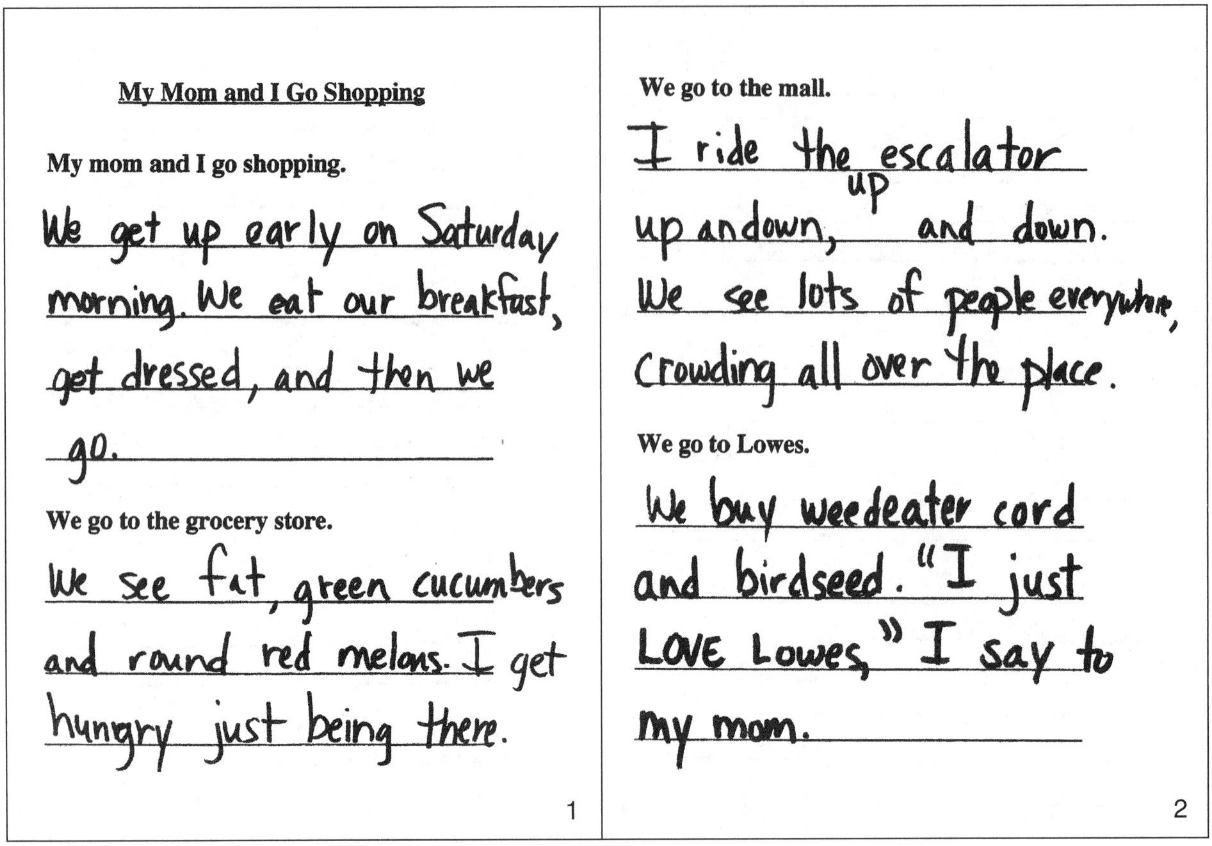

My Mom and I Go Shopping

My mom and I go shopping.

We get up early on Saturday morning. We eat our breakfast, get dressed, and then we go.

We go to the grocery store.

We see fat, green cucumbers and round red melons. I get hungry just being there.

1

We go to the mall.

I ride the escalator up and down, up and down.

We see lots of people everywhere, crowding all over the place.

We go to Lowes.

We buy weedeater cord and birdseed. "I just LOVE Lowes," I say to my mom.

2

FIGURE K.2 Katie does some revision work as a demonstration.

interaction together and think about how they might try it when they revise. This kind of peer conference will feel familiar to them if we've studied peer conferencing earlier in the year. The difference is that now they are learning a more specific way to help with the writing. Some of them choose to do their revision work with others, and many of them do it on their own.

When we finally send them out to revise, the actual work of it goes very quickly. They usually revise an entire piece in this way in one day—with time to spare to work on something else! We may decide to have them do more than one piece, or we may just go straight to looking at what everyone did with his or her revisions and celebrating our smart work. When we share their revisions, we like to read each piece once as it was before the author made any additions and then read it again in its revised form. We talk then about the difference the revision made. This processing talk after the children revise is absolutely essential to the study, as it helps them grab hold of what they have done as writers.

Some of the children will choose to completely remake their books and include the revisions and all new illustrations, but most don't, and we don't require them to do this. Our goal is to teach young writers to

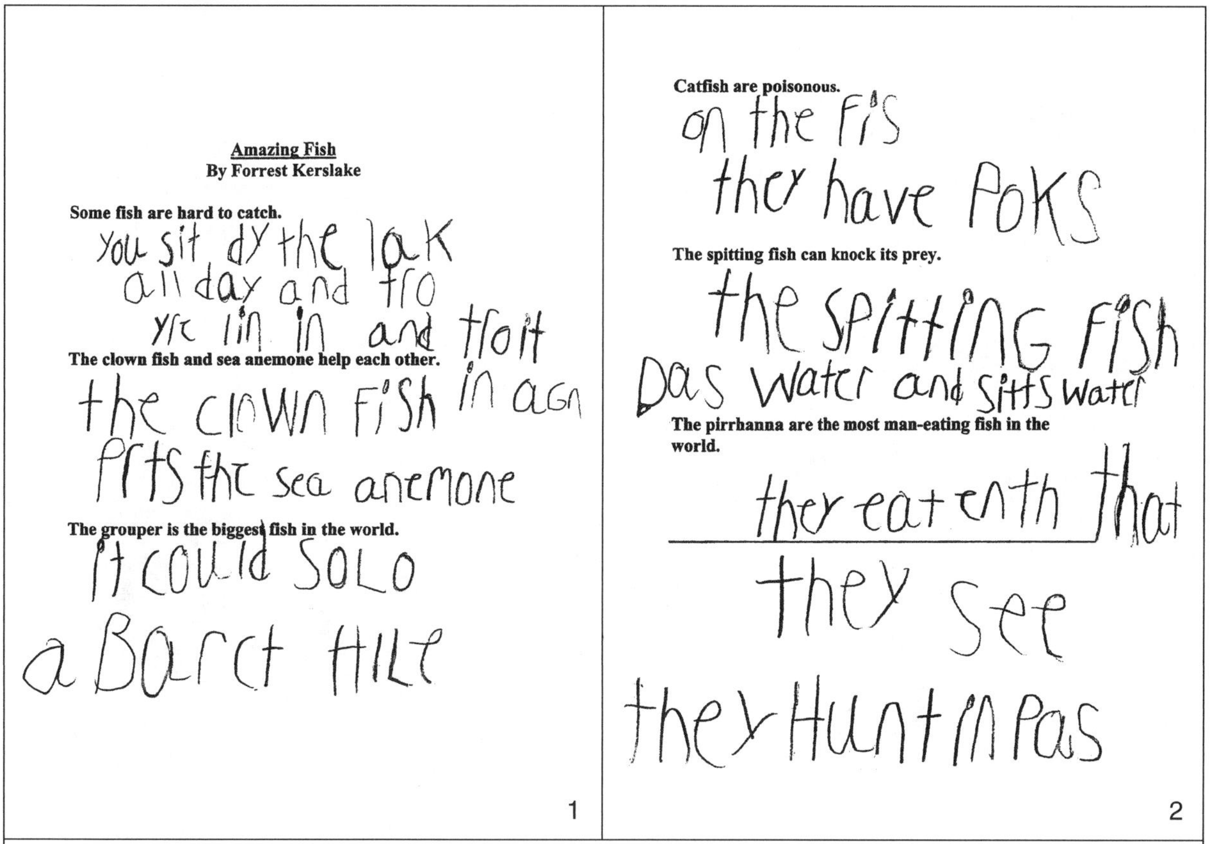

Amazing Fish
By Forrest Kerslake

Some fish are hard to catch.

you sit dy the lak
all day and fro
yrc lin in and troit
in agn

The clown fish and sea anemone help each other.

the clown fish
Prts the sea anemone

The grouper is the biggest fish in the world.

It could solo
a Barct Hile

1

Catfish are poisonous.

on the fis
ther have Poks

The spitting fish can knock its prey.

the spitting fish
Das water and sitts water

The pirrhanna are the most man-eating fish in the world.

ther eat enth that
they see
they Hunt in Pas

2

Key for Forrest's "Amazing Fish" revisions

Some fish are hard to catch.
You sit by the lake
all day and throw
your line in and throw it
          in again.

The clown fish and sea anemone
help each other.
The clown fish
protects the sea anemone.

The grouper is the biggest fish in the world.
It could swallow
a barracuda whole.

Catfish are poisonous.
On the fins
they have pokes.

The spitting fish can knock
its prey.
The spitting fish drinks water and
spits water.

The piranha are the most man-
eating fish in the world.
They eat anything that
they see.
They hunt in packs.

3

FIGURE K.3 Forrest revises his *Amazing Fish* book.

FIGURE K.4 Helena revises her book about dogs.

Dogs can
Run fistue
with teRwue
legs and Dogs
licu.

Some Dogs
are Yellow
and TaYue
siCue teRwue
Tuese out.

5

6

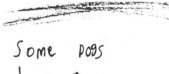

Some Dogs
have Black
SRiPSeu

7

FIGURE K.4 *continued*

A Book About Dogs
By Helena Hunt

A dog lives in a dog house and dogs can scratch.

they live in their cozy house where they sleep at nihgt. and dog's scrach with their sharp claw wach out **they miet** scrach you.

Dogs can bite with their sharp teeth.

their sharp teeth can some times make your skin bleed. wach out they miet Biet your finger of.

Dogs can run and dogs bark.

they run with their long leg's and they run fast. and they bark with. their wide open math.

8

Dogs can run faster with their legs and dogs lick.

they have four leg's thats why their leg's make them go fast. and they lick with their stickey tongue.

Some dogs are yellow and they stick their tongues out.

their fur is yellow but not their bold body. dog's stick their tongue out whe their makeing a noise.

Some dogs have black stripes.

their black stripes can not come of because babie's some times think that they can come of and they try to pul them of and it is funny!

9

FIGURE K.4 *continued*

go through the process of revision and to learn from going through that process. While we expect their writing will get better as a result of this work, our goal is not better books. Our goal is better writers.

Before getting out of the study, we want to be sure we come back to the big idea of revision as revisiting a piece you like so much that you want to stay with it. We want to think with the children about how revision can become a natural part of their future work. Because we have chosen to do this study at the very end of the year, we don't have much of an opportunity to follow up and begin asking students about revision in their future work. We *could* do the study earlier in the year, especially if we feel our writers are fluent and confident and ready to begin thinking about revision in beginning ways. If we did, we would certainly then follow it out into their work and expect them to use these revision strategies from time to time in their writing.

Resources for Getting Started

Here are three more quotes from writers about revision that are appropriate for our youngest writers. Be sure to show the children some of the writer's work if he or she is unfamiliar to them.

Naomi Shihab Nye: "I STRONGLY advise that you read your work out loud to yourself as you revise it. No need to feel foolish. The best writers do this, and it will help you more than anything else." From Paul B. Janeczko (ed.), *Seeing the Blue Between: Advice and Inspiration for Young Poets* (Cambridge, MA: Candlewick, 2002), 87.

Connection: Suggest the children try this as they are thinking about what to add. They can read their pieces aloud and see what naturally comes out as a possible addition.

Georgia Heard: "Sometimes I try to pretend that I am a stranger reading my writing and I ask myself if it would be clear to another person if she read my words." From Georgia Heard, *The Revision Toolbox* (Portsmouth, NH: Heinemann, 2002), 75.

Connection: Suggest the children try reading their pieces like strangers and asking themselves, "What else do I know about this that a stranger wouldn't know?"

Mem Fox: "If I didn't talk about my writing, how would I know what to improve? In fact, rewriting is often synonymous with retalking to anyone who will listen." From Mem Fox, *Dear Mem Fox, I Have Read All Your Books Even the Pathetic Ones and Other Incidents in the Life of a Children's Book Author* (San Diego: Harcourt Brace Jovanovich, 1992), 166.

Connection: Retalking! If children want to use a partner to help them do this revision work, they may find someone and retalk their writing, just as Mem does.

Closing Thoughts

Writing a book like this, we find ourselves thinking often of the people we hope will someday read it. We imagine a teacher at a conference, standing at a table full of professional books for sale, thumbing quickly through the pages of this book. We imagine that the first thing that might capture this teacher's attention are the children's writing samples sprinkled throughout the book. We imagine this teacher might think to herself, "Well, this sure looks like the writing my first graders do." We imagine she might wonder at someone writing yet another book about what looks like ordinary first-grade writing. We imagine she might long for a book that explains how to help young children do something somehow different than ordinary first-grade writing—maybe something a little neater or with a little more volume.

About the Authors: Writing Workshop with Our Youngest Writers is not the book she longs for. We imagine that if you have read through this entire book and reached these closing thoughts, you know that. You know that we have no secret formulas, no magic potions, which will help our youngest writers gain fluency and control over written language more quickly. We don't know how to help them *not* write like six-year-olds, and as you might imagine, we have no desire to help them *not* write like six-years-olds. Why would we want them to do that? You see, we believe in them as six-year-olds.

We believe that while their writing may look ordinary, what we know *about the authors* is always quite extraordinary. What we know *about the authors*, who find ideas and choose topics and fill a whole year of their lives with writing, is quite extraordinary. What we know *about the authors*, who understand that they can make decisions as they write, that they can craft with purpose and intention, is quite extraordinary. What we know *about the authors*, who stun us with their ever-emerging insights about the wonderful promise of written language, is quite extraordinary.

Our greatest wish for our teaching is that we will always have the knowing eyes to see how extraordinary the authors really are. Our greatest wish for this book is that it will help others see this, too.

Works Cited

Alarcón, Francisco X. 1997. *Laughing Tomatoes and Other Spring Poems / Jitomates Risueños y Otros Poemas de Primavera*. Illus. by Maya Christina Gonzalez. San Francisco: Children's Book.

Angelillo, Janet. 2002. *A Fresh Approach to Teaching Punctuation*. New York: Scholastic.

Asch, Frank. 1994. *The Earth and I*. New York: Harcourt Brace.

————. 1995. *Water*. New York: Harcourt.

Calkins, Lucy, and colleagues. 2003. *Units of Study for Primary Writing: A Yearlong Curriculum (K–2)*. Portsmouth, NH: Firsthand.

Copeland, Jeffrey S. 1993. *Speaking of Poets: Interviews with Poets Who Write for Young Children*. Urbana, IL: National Council of Teachers of English.

Crews, Donald. 1995. *Sail Away*. New York: Harper Trophy.

Fisher, Valorie. 2002. *My Big Brother*. New York: Atheneum Books for Young Readers.

Graham, Bob. 2001. *"Let's Get a Pup!" Said Kate*. Cambridge, MA: Candlewick.

Gray, Libba Moore. 1995. *My Mama Had a Dancing Heart*. London, England: Orchard Books.

Karas, G. Brian. 2002. *Atlantic*. New York: G. P. Putnam's Sons.

Kurtz, Jane, and Christopher Kurtz. 2002. *Water Hole Waiting*. Illus. by Lee Christiansen. New York: Greenwillow.

Laminack, Lester, and Katie Wood. 1996. *Spelling in Use: Looking Closely at Spelling in Whole Language Classrooms*. Urbana, IL: National Council of Teachers of English.

Lindbergh, Reeve. 1994. *What Is the Sun?* Illus. by Stephen Lambert. Cambridge, MA: Candlewick.

Marcus, Leonard, ed. 2000. *Author Talk.* New York: Simon and Schuster.

Murray, Donald. 1990. *Shoptalk: Learning to Write with Writers.* Portsmouth, NH: Heinemann.

The North Carolina Standard Course of Study. North Carolina Department of Public Instruction.

Raschka, Christopher. 1998. *Yo! Yes?* London, England: Orchard Books.

———. 2000. *Ring! Yo?* New York: DK Publishing.

Ray, Katie Wood. 1999. *Wondrous Words: Writers and Writing in the Elementary Classroom.* Urbana, IL: National Council of Teachers of English.

Ray, Katie Wood, with Lester Laminack. 2001. *The Writing Workshop: Working Through the Hard Parts (and They're All Hard Parts).* Urbana, IL: National Council of Teachers of English.

Ryder, Joanne. 1996. *Earthdance.* Illus. by Norman Gorbaty. New York: Henry Holt.

Rylant, Cynthia. 1998. *Scarecrow.* Illus. by Lauren Stringer. New York: Harcourt Brace.

———. 2000. *The Wonderful Happens.* New York: Simon and Schuster.

———. 2002. *Christmas in the Country.* Illus. by Diane Goode. New York: Blue Sky.

Yolen, Jane. n.d. "Jane Yolen's Interview Transcript." Retrieved from *www2.scholastic.com/teachers/authorsandbooks/authorstudies /authorhome.jhtml?authorID=215&collateralID=6664&displayName =Interview+Transcript.*

Zolotow, Charlotte. 1995. *When the Wind Stops.* Illus. by Stefano Vitale. New York: HarperTrophy.

Index